Praise for Psychedelic Wild Child

"Dawn Hurwitz' story of her wild, idealistic, searching journey in the 1970s and her time with Father Yod and The Source Family is lusty, loving, raw, and real. Her utter lack of inhibition in her life and in her storytelling gives this book a feeling of deep authenticity that becomes its greatest power." — *Jodi Wille, book publisher, author, and Director of* The Source Family *documentary*

"Thanks to this unabashedly intimate memoir, we finally have answers to the lingering questions and preconceived notions that have swirled around the mythology of The Source Family and its charismatic yet polarizing leader, Father Yod.

In this astonishing narrative, Galaxy the Aquarian, birth name Dawn Hurwitz, a sexually, spiritually, and intellectually rebellious Jewish teenager of 16 boldly turns her back on mainstream life in the pursuit of cosmic love and enlightenment, becoming the youngest among thirteen wives to Father Yod, a man in his 50s.

A deeply sensual memoir of desire—for sex, transcendence, and eventually, money's "green energy"—it reveals how Dawn, like so many seekers, pays a high price for daring to step outside the confines that society imposed upon women of that era (and today). As we follow in her determined footsteps, we gain unprecedented and meticulously detailed insights into the inner workings of The Source—a social experiment where daily life was an intricate dance involving the quest for cosmic wisdom, wholesome living, and an ever-evolving, unconventional romantic paradigm.

Dawn emerges as an archetypal Icarus in feminine form, single-mindedly focused on one objective—to be as close as possible to her spiritual mentor, and object of her desire, Father Yod. Time and time again, she flies too close to his fire, finally plummeting back to a harsh reality following his untimely death in 1975.

As Yod's exciting, far-out Patriarchy morphs uneasily into a Matriarchy led by his grieving wives, Dawn finds herself at the bottom of a totem pole she no longer desires to climb. Not for the first time in her life, she rebels against a system that is caging her, becoming the first of Yod's wives to leave the family. Re-entering the modern world with nothing but memories and her alluring figure, she finds herself lured into sex work by a former satellite member of the Family, who becomes her pimp and psychological jailor, until she finds the strength within herself to finally break free.

Despite the adversity Hurwitz endured as a result of devoting herself to The Source, she has no regrets, making a compelling case for reframing the group as less of a "cult" and more a "cultural reform movement." Nearly five decades since seeing Father Yod's unearthly blue gaze for the first time, she paints a vivid picture of a genuinely wild psychedelic ride, an adventure in communal living, one where love, trust, and the quest for ineffable truth—and not brainwashing—served as the binding forces that kept these beautiful dreamers together." — *Caroline Ryder, Journalist,* LA Times, Dazed magazine

Psychedelic
WILD CHILD

Coming of Age
IN THE
Source Family
Cult{ure}

Dawn "Galaxy" Hurwitz

Psychedelic Wild Child: Coming of Age in the Source Family Cult{ure}
Copyright © 2023 by Dawn Hurwitz

First Edition

This work depicts actual events in the life of the author as truthfully as recollection permits and/or can be verified by research. Occasionally, dialogue consistent with the character or nature of the person speaking has been supplemented. All persons within are actual individuals; there are no composite characters.

Cover Design by Fresh Design
Cover Painting owned by Dawn Hurwitz, artist uknown
Interior Typesetting by Melissa Williams Design
Author Painting by Arthur Johnsen

No part of this publication may be used or reproduced in any manner whatsoever without written permission, except in the case of brief quotations embodied in critical articles, or reviews, or for teaching purposes.

ISBN: 979-8-9885130-0-1 (ebook)
ISBN: 979-8-9885130-1-8 (paperback)
ISBN: 979-8-9885130-2-5 (hardcover)

Names: Hurwitz, Dawn, 1956- .
Title: Psychedelic wild child : coming of age in The Source Family cult{ure} / Dawn "Galaxy" Hurwitz.
Description: [Pahoa, HI] : Speck in Sky Publications, 2023. | Summary: Dawn Hurwitz left Chicago at age sixteen, landing in Los Angeles and joining The Source Family vegetarian commune led by Father Yod. Eventually moving to Hawaii in quest of a utopian lifestyle, the group loses it all in a surprising turn of events, while Dawn discovers her own personal power.
Identifiers: LCCN 2023913181 | ISBN 9798988513025 (hardcover) | ISBN 9798988513018 (pbk.) | ISBN 9798988513001 (epub)
Subjects: LCSH: Hurwitz, Dawn, 1956 -. | Ya Ho Wha, 1922-1975. | Source Family (Cult). | Communal living – California – Los Angeles. | Cults – California – Los Angeles. | Cults – Hawaii. | BISAC: BIOGRAPHY & AUTOBIOGRAPHY / Personal Memoirs. | BIOGRAPHY & AUTOBIOGRAPHY / Women.
Classification: LCC HQ971.5.L67 .H87 2023 (print) | DDC 920.H--dc23
LC record available at https://lccn.loc.gov/2023913181

Psychedelic
WILD CHILD

Coming of Age
IN THE
Source Family
Cult{ure}

For Stephen

Contents

Los Angeles: Sunset Strip, 1973	8
Preface	10
1—Arrival	14
2—In the Beginning	16
3—Rogers Park	19
4—Summoning Revolution	26
5—Firsts	31
6—Sex & Drugs & Rock'n'Roll Summer of 1970	36
7—The Last Gasps of Domesticity	46
8—The Conjuring	50
9—Dawnlight of the Age of Aquarian	58
10—Finding My Spiritual Father	63
11—Dawnlight Sheds on Bonadea	69
12—Living in LA, The Source Way	74
13—All Fall Down	83
14—And Then There Were Five	89
15—Here Today, Gone to Maui	94
16—Paradise Lost, Dreaming Anew	104
17—New Era LA: The Father House	108
18—Becoming One	113
19—Source Family Style	117
20—Being with Yahowha	128
21—Kauai	133
22—Roots of Disillusionment	138

23—The Atherton Mansion	145
24—On the Road Again	149
25—The Startling Truth	154
26—Suspended Animation	158
27—Wandering	164
28—Threading a New Needle	173
29—The House of the Sun Rising	179
30—Running in the Fast Lane	185
31—Chinatown	190
32—Pretty Maids All in a Row	196
33—Into the Dark, Deep End	201
34—Gasping for Air	206
35—Twenty-Third Birthday	208
36—Regrouping	212
37—Checkmate	219
38—Aloha, Honolulu	223
Epilogue	228
Acknowledgments	231
About the Author	233

Los Angeles
Sunset Strip
1973

I distracted myself by getting more shifts at The Source Restaurant; it gave me an opportunity to have close encounters with Father Yod, which I took full advantage of, as we all did. I spent all my spare time listening to his wisdom—sometimes even when I was supposed to be working. Father looked happy to see me whenever I popped in.

One day while upstairs of the Source on a break, Father and I found ourselves alone. This was not unusual, as people came and went upstairs all the time. We would talk with him about any problems we had, discuss things we might not understand or, as in my case, just come to hang on his every word. We all clustered around him to listen.

He was sitting in full lotus with his long silver and gold locks tumbling over his shoulders and a shawl wrapped around him. His back was to the altar, and he spoke of something he'd read in a book. "It's over in that stack," he said as he pointed across the room. "Would you fetch it for me?"

I recall wearing a long, white gown, in a lightweight T-shirt fabric, suspended from my shoulders by a lace yoke just above my breasts. Because the ceiling was very low in that corner of the room, I crawled over to retrieve the book. I moved slowly and deliberately, like a cat. What was I doing? It felt very sexy, and I enjoyed it. I could feel his eyes following me, enjoying my grace. I dug through the stack, picked *out the volume, turned, and caught his brilliant blue gaze while slowly returning.*

He was mesmerized. Reaching for the book I was handing him, he brought me closer. I wedged into his lap, which was not unusual; he often gave us hugs seated that way. His hand touched my face, and I leaned in and nuzzled his soft, silver beard. Our lips met. This was heaven. I dissolved in his embrace.

After a few minutes he asked, "Would you like to move in up here with me?"

"Yes, would I ever, Father!" My ears were zinging, along with every cell in my body!

"You can call me 'Yod,' now that we are to be lovers."

"But what about Ahom? She's your wife. Aren't the man and his woman one?"

"We are one, and I am also one with you."

He looked at me with tenderness as I accepted his resolve.

Preface

In the Sixties, the counterculture mounted an unbridled search for truth, righteousness, and a feeling of belonging. Driven by the need to reinvent what they often couldn't find at home, many joined communes all over the country.

Timothy Miller wrote in his book; *The 60s Communes: Hippies and Beyond* (Syracuse Studies on Peace and Conflict Resolution), Syracuse University Press, 1999:

> Communal societies have long been an American cultural fixture, with anywhere from dozens to hundreds of them operating at any given moment since the pioneers of Plockhoy's Commonwealth and the Labadists of Bohemia Manor took to the common life in the seventeenth century. Nothing in the American communal past, however, would have led any judicious observer to predict the incredible communal explosion that began during the 1960s. In a period of just a few years communal fever gripped the alienated youth of the United States—indeed, of the developed world—and thousands upon thousands of new communities were established throughout the land. The size and diversity of the new communitarianism made accurate counting of communes and of their members impossible, but the overall significance of the 1960s era (here defined as 1960 to 1975, inclusive) as a watershed in American communal history is undeniable.

I too found myself on that journey for truth, for something to believe in that made sense in my soul. During the summer of 1972, I found it in Los Angeles with the Source Family.

Dawn Hurwitz

Father Yod, later Yahowha, was our spiritual Father who shared with us the truth we were seeking. He had a way of blending knowledge from many different beliefs—Kabbalistic, Christian, Buddhist, Rosicrucian, Zarathustran. Whatever source he read from, he found truth within it. Never following those paths hook, line, and sinker, he would glean for us the essence of truth we could apply in our lives. He was creating a living experiment. Within the Source Family, we would use what worked and discard the rest.

Without culture, humankind has no society, no celebration of creativity, productivity, or compassionate belief. While there are many systems of belief all over the world and through time, some have been relegated as cults. They were never able to gain the following more widespread beliefs received. Although some of them have been good and righteous in their own creeds, others have been more dubious. So why is it that if it's considered a cult, it's known as a bad thing today? After all, 'cult' is just the root term of 'culture.'

I guess Charles Manson, the Jonestown Massacre, the Branch Davidians, and Heaven's Gate played a role in that. These groups did not have respect for life, and their charismatic leaders did not teach them to think for themselves. But this is really no different than some of the ancient Romans or even some of the modern megalomaniacs. And how about all the Christian explorers who destroyed cultures they deemed primitive, like the Native Americans, upon whose soil American citizens now proudly sit? Or the African nations, strong in their tribal and family ties, who were told that if they didn't bow down to Jesus, their lives were empty? And even today, we have the Catholic Church, which has been plagued by child abuse for years. It is not known as a bad cult, just a barrel with a few bad apples.

Some may have head-scratching elements, but we are throwing the baby out with the bathwater to consign all modern cults as bad. So I'm going to have to stand up for what I know.

Many years have passed since the Source Family unraveled. Some members have stayed friends, while most of us have drifted. Yet the majority are still positive about the experience we've shared, and I've kept in touch with many over the years. I've gleefully observed their blossoming into human beings who've integrated themselves into the world, using all of the positive ideas we learned from Yahowha as a base to stand on. They have become doctors, creatives, business professionals, and parents of beautiful children.

Others have turned against what they learned and never want to see our shared involvement as something that was a positive force in their lives. This is how life goes. Not everyone has the same experience. Not everyone is happy. We all have our burdens and choose our own paths.

Lately, I feel even more adrift from my so-called brothers and sisters of the Source. I am grateful to have spent my life developing rational thought and compassion. I take responsibility for my own experience and accept whatever has happened and my role within it. I know that I choose my involvement, and mostly at this point, I choose not to be involved at all. This has baffled some Source Family members so much that they refuse me permission to even mention their names, which is really a shame. So some of the names here have been changed.

I do have very fond memories of most of the five years I spent with them. And I have fond memories of the time before, which brought me to them. I hope you enjoy my journey.

1
Arrival

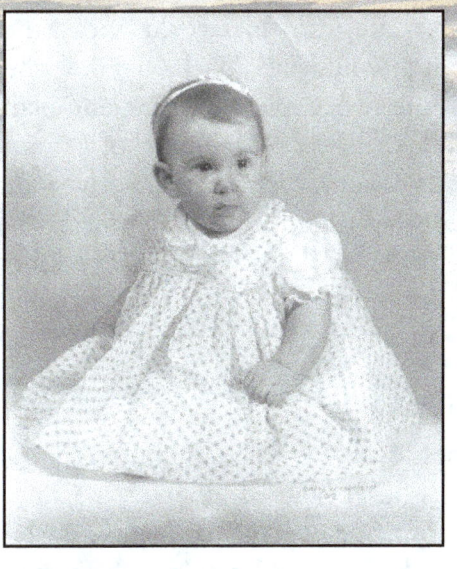

"Wait . . . what?! Oh, no! I have to do this all over again?! I was hoping not to repeat this. Yet here I am. In this body of a tiny girl. And I have no control over it. I can't remember what got me here. It's like waking from a dream; I can almost see flashing glimpses of what happened, but the scene slips away like shifting clouds. What didn't I get right?

"Oh, all right. Here I go! I've got to give up questioning and try again. If only I could recall why!"

I do know now. I know in my gut. I know in my soul. I know we all reincarnate from one form to another. Can I prove it? Not a chance. But I know it as I look at that picture of me as a babe, sitting propped up, *tiny fists clenched, placed in that dotted dress with tight, puffy sleeves. That look of frustration on my face says it all: "What am I doing here? Why is this happening to me?" They tried to put a ribbon around my head, to make me pretty. They tried to make me comfortable. But how could I be? Back in a body, on earth, sensing the changing times to come? I would have to pioneer, take part in spearheading a movement of spirituality, equality, change. No one would be telling me what to do. And they all wanted to tell me what to do.*

"Nope! I know what to do—I know it by instinct. I'll get it right this time, and I'll get off this planet!"

△ ▽ △ ▽

My mother says I came into this world with a mission. My grandmother mused that I would already be awake when she awoke, just sitting by myself, quietly occupied, plotting and planning. My teachers always had to check that box on the back of my report card that said, "Does not follow directions." I was as self-driven and stubborn as they come. Yep, they got that right! But it didn't mean I had no compassion, that I didn't want to share, that I would not be kind.

Okay, there were those moments. I couldn't explain why I had that outburst, why I ran ahead of the crowd, why I left. I couldn't help myself: I had someplace to go and something to do. It was bigger than anything else. Others found it hard to keep up with me. I didn't fit into the normal molds. It wasn't possible; I couldn't. But I took responsibility for my actions. I never blamed others.

Mother let me run. She knew I'd come home. Maybe a little bruised, maybe a little late. But I would return. My intuition was my guide; there was no other way. I chose this path. Somehow, I would learn my lessons with this family, with these circumstances. And whenever I did not listen to my sixth sense, things went badly. I would have to do it all over again.

Today I've come to terms with my lot in life. Now that I can see them from afar, I need to dig up these many trials to see how the puzzle pieces all fit together.

Before I get so far away that I can't see them anymore.

2

In the Beginning

Standing in the alley behind our brick apartment building, I gripped the towering chain-link fence isolating me from the schoolyard. I watched in fascination as the sun cast crimson shadows under the dusky summer sky. The warm air slowly shifted blue into purple as the light faded. My foot shuffled back and forth on the gravel, kicking the little stones through the fence while I watched the kids climbing the monkey bars far on the other side of it. I wanted to play with the older kids on that playground, do the things I was told I was too young for.

Suddenly, an unknown dark sensation rushed toward me with a dense, invisible force. It sucked all the air away and replaced it with fear and dread. I could barely make out the huge, deep-gray head emerging. Its sinister grin smoldered as it floated nearer. I snapped out of this rush of horror and ran as fast as those four-year-old legs would go. Back down the alley, flying up the winding wooden back stairs to our first-floor porch. I came safely through the back door, slamming it behind me and escaping that sinister shadow of doom, standing with my back to the door, panting. This is my earliest memory.

Of course, my parents thought I was being overly imaginative. "Some things just can't be explained," said Audrey, my mother. Later, we cuddled on her bed as she read me stories from Edith Hamilton's *Greek Mythology* to illustrate that fact, as well as how myths could tell the stories of the world we occupy.

This was a first glimpse of the supernatural in my little world. And ever since, a quest for the unknown has been the soundtrack of my life. It's led to an insatiable search to figure out where we come from and how everything works. Whoever has made us, *and* who made them? I've yearned to know infinitely more, go deeper, far below the surface of everything. What does it all mean? These inquiries and instincts have consumed my life, compounding a bottomless quest for truth.

I used to have a repetitive dream as a child. I would become helplessly tangled up and lost in God's file-cabinet drawers. While floating in space, the huge metal drawers would appear the size of a building. God would not be there, but I would know this space was his. I would slip inside a drawer left ajar. Hovering in the air around me would be dozens of room-sized balls of yarn in deep shades of blues, greens, and golds. Colored, metallic knitting needles would be stuck through the balls. Loose, thick end strands of soft yarn would drift weightlessly around. As I floated around them, the ends clung to me. It made me feel so small, insignificant, and captured, as if in a spiderweb. How would I get out of this? And then I would wake up—a useful trick I have resorted to throughout my life of random, weird dreams.

Staring out at the infinity of night stars invokes the same feeling of profound randomness. Why am I here? What is my mission? Have I always wanted to be more than just a speck in the sky, to stand out in some way and for some reason, like a comet or falling star? But why?

One winter's day when I was about seven, I was leaning over the back of the couch, staring out the front window of our first-floor apartment and watching big, gently falling snowflakes. I loved watching the snow decorate the trees, bushes, walkways, and cars, and wondered at the beauty of it all. I saw my dad walk out the front door of the building downstairs holding Danny by the hand, who was bundled up looking something like a stuffed toy. He picked Danny up, and they got into Dad's white Rambler at the curb and drove off.

"Mom, Danny and Dad just left. Where did they go?" I yelled, feeling like I was missing out on something.

"Dad's in the back room watching TV, and Danny is on his rocking horse," Mother yelled back. She walked into the living room with a quizzical look on her face while wiping her hands on a kitchen towel. "What are you talking about?"

"Mom, I watched them, right here from the window! They drove down the street. I know it was them! Danny was standing in the back seat right behind Dad like he always does, holding Dad's shoulder! I saw it plain as day."

Mother laughed. "No, that's impossible! They're in the back of the apartment. They haven't gone anywhere."

I've never been able to figure that one out. To this moment I can see them in my mind's eye, driving down the snow-covered street, Danny standing in the back seat, stuffed into his white snowsuit and mittens, and tied up in his red-and-blue knit scarf. It must have been a multi-dimensional moment, one of those times that made me question if life is as it seems. Was there more than what we were being taught in school?

In the background, the fence of the alley, and the building we lived in. This is mother's family when she was 7 in front of Field School.

3

Rogers Park

Audrey & Dick

The farthest north you can go in the city of Chicago is the neighborhood of Rogers Park. My parents grew up there after their parents and other Jewish families migrated from the west-side city settlements to establish a new, safer Jewish community.

    My mother, Audrey, was a tall, popular beauty, with piercing, hazel eyes, and wavy, blond hair. As a child of the Depression, her parents taught her how to keep strong values and get along. They witnessed the Holocaust from afar, grateful for their freedom but hesitant to make waves. So Audrey learned to fit in and not be noticed. In the spring of 1955, my father, Dick, was twenty-five years old and near to being discharged from the Air Force. A dark, handsome ladies' man, he always had a twinkle in his eye, was very sure of himself, and cut a fine, fit figure in uniform. He would spend three days on and then three off at the Air Force base in Williams Bay just north of Chicago. On his off days, he would return to Chicago to get some flight time in at O'Hare Field. He was searching for the next step in his life.

When Audrey met Dick, she sensed he was a handful and too much trouble. But she'd always had a problem saying no. An easygoing dreamer, Audrey did what everyone else wanted to—including Dick. But they did both have something in common: they both loved music. Eventually, she began taking trips to spend overnight with him at the base, and later that year, she became pregnant.

It was a time when people settled down, married, and had children. There was no question that my parents would marry. Publicly, their anniversary was celebrated one month earlier than their actual wedding date, allowing me to be born exactly nine months later. My sister Amy followed after fourteen months, and my father would have to wait another five years for a son, Danny.

Amy ran by my side in everything—whether she wanted to or not—though I believed she wanted to. She just would never do on her own the outrageous things I would get up to, like crossing the alleys and streets, and traveling outside our boundaries. We were very close.

Technology was an early interest. Me, Dad, and Amy.

Danny was a hyperactive, mischievous kid, yet doted on by everyone. Because his energy matched mine, we often provoked each other. He had a sweet smile that endeared him till it turned impish. Encouraged by my father in all sports, he could often be heard pretending to be the announcer of a hockey game, sliding down our polished wood-floored hallways in his stockinged feet and coming to a crashing halt at the end yelling, "Goal!" as he smashed into the wall. Our Danny boy!

Because I was the oldest, my parents entrusted me with the care of my younger siblings, hoping I would set an example for them. I tried but was often distracted by the enticement of things I was told not to do, which looked like much more fun. It's something my sister will never forgive me for and my brother is ever humored by. In fact, as I grew, rules became just fences of words. If they made no sense to me, they had to be tested, rationalized—and often broken. I had to find out for myself. Many a time, this bought me more than I'd bargained for. Why couldn't I go down to the beach in the winter alone? I longed to witness that silent, placid stretch of nature, frozen and blanketed in white. Why couldn't I join those boys who liked to play war in the construction lots when the weather warmed up? I was just as strong and rugged as they were. Why were the bad boys the ones I wanted to play with? They did all the exciting, fun stuff. Even though I was forbidden, that somehow never stopped me. I was taken advantage of more than once because of my careless curiosity.

My adventurous nature revealed itself in other ways too. Once, my mother caught me with a pair of scissors, "fringing" the bottom of the green linen curtains she had so painstakingly appliquéd with matching floral fabric from our bedspreads. I marveled at my power to make all those little snips, how they changed the fabric. Recognizing my developing creative streak, my mother exposed me to the arts. She knew I needed to channel that energy, so she made sure I took all kinds of classes to infuse and direct that creative impulse. I loved it, so much so that it became a driving passion—beginning with dressing up my Troll doll tribe in anything I could make from the scraps of my mother's sewing box, and later in life, becoming a clothing and costume designer.

Some might assume I was born to a life of privilege, having wealthy Jewish parents who gave me everything. It's a partial truth. My family was comfortable but not rich in dollars. There was an actual middle class in those days, but we were on the lower fringe of it. Our wealth was born of my parents' pragmatic dedication to their family. They embraced the idea that people can be whatever they want to make of themselves if they work for it and have the confidence and focus to accomplish it. Dad gave up his dreams to be a pilot and went to work with his father selling used machinery. Mom stayed home and raised the kids. We had little extra money. Dad worked hard for it and we lived in rental apartments till I was eleven. He became the first member of his family to own a home, something his parents would never accomplish.

I grew up in three different apartments near the lake. I have no recall of the first one, where I was born, but do have great memories of the latter two. In those days trust was not an issue. When I was old enough to go to school, I could finally wander to the schoolyard around the corner to play on the swings and monkey bars, but I had to take Amy and Danny with me. The playground was visible from our back porch across other yards and felt safe enough for my parents to be able to spy on us. We could clearly hear Dad at the back door, yelling at the top of his lungs with his hands cupped around his mouth, "Didi, Amy, Danny, dinner!" He would wait until he saw us running, and he usually didn't have to yell twice.

Mondoo and Doogee

In the early sixties, beatniks would emerge. They were called this based on the experimental jazz and folk music they listened to, and their counterculture blossomed with artists and writers. I would see them once in a while walking through the neighborhood with their longer, unkempt hair and beards, and their black clothing—especially turtle-necked pullovers, dark sunglasses, and felt berets.

Mostly, the beatniks were on their way to a noted coffeehouse down the street called the No Exit Cafe. It was like their headquarters. The floor-to-ceiling windows allowed a view of the shabby wooden tables and chairs, an old, upright piano, some music stands and microphones, and a little stage by a black wall. A chalkboard menu listed coffee, pastries, and sandwiches. It always smelled like smoke, the ashtrays on the tables heaving in evidence. People sat around reading, playing chess, and having revolutionary conversations, according to my mother.

At the time, my Aunt Jackie had moved into an apartment building across the street from us, where Jack and Judy, a beatnik couple, lived. One day, I spied them walking their dogs down the street and flew down the stairs to meet them. Bursting out of the front door, we suddenly stood eye to eye.

"Hi! My name is Didi. I love your doggies. I've been watching them from my window upstairs. What kind are they?" I babbled.

"Hi, Didi. I'm Jack. This is my wife, Judy, and the dogs are Dachshunds," answered Jack, amused.

Judy wasn't very talkative and practically whispered a hushed "hello" in a deep, almost raspy voice. She stared out from behind dark, narrow rectangular sunglasses slipping down her nose. With shadowy makeup rimming her eyes, long, straight, jet hair, and tight black pants and boots, she resembled Morticia from the Addams family. Draped in a Mexican-blanket poncho and jeans, Jack stood almost a head shorter than Judy and looked a little like my father, with dark hair and eyes. His face was dominated by a bold, bushy mustache, and his hair curled over his ears, brushing below his collar. Jack was a little more animated in a laid-back way, but seemed kind, patient, and humored by my exuberance.

"Can I pet them?" I begged, and before they could even answer, I was down on my knees rubbing the dogs' excited heads as they licked me in greeting.

"Tell me their names!"

"Mondoo and Doogee," Jack laughed.

I thought he laughed because they were unusual names, so I laughed too. That's how it all started. We became friends, and I would race down the stairs with Amy and Danny in chase if we saw Jack and Judy from the window. But there was always a little unspoken reserve from my parents when the couple was around.

We often met down at the beach in the summertime, clustered on lounge chairs and conversing in the grassy area above the sand. Aunt Jackie came down too, chatting away, as usual. Jack and Judy were fascinating to me because they were so unlike anyone I knew.

A couple of years after Jack and Judy moved away, Dad received a couple of weird phone calls. One was from a casino in Las Vegas, wondering when he was going to pay his marker. Another was from Indiana, requesting payment for the car he'd bought. Dad brushed these off as wrong numbers that had nothing to do with him.

Some months later he discovered some misinformation on the forms he received while filing his taxes. He hadn't made any money from a job in San Diego! Then, after failing to receive his tax-return money, he discovered to his astonishment that the check had been sent in his name to a San Diego address! On top of that, when he tried to renew his passport, he was told there was a hold on it—and there was a warrant for his arrest from the Israeli government! It seems a man named Jack Katz had stolen his identity! And not only his but my mother's and little brother Danny's identities too. Apparently, Judy had had a son with another man who was loaded and had custody of him. Jack and Judy were going to use my brother's identity so they could leave the country with the boy.

In the sixties, identity theft was in its infancy. If you had a little of the right information—for instance, a mother's maiden name and address—you were taken on your word when applying for a duplicate Social Security card. With that in hand, you could get a duplicate driver's license. And with that combination, you could apply for a passport. It had helped that Jack resembled my father so much. It had also helped that the couple had gotten so friendly with Aunt Jackie, who had provided them with all of our family's intimate details, thinking she was just having casual conversations.

Jack got busted in Israel for trying to sell the passport with my dad's name on it. While awaiting trial, he left the country using his own passport. It took Dad years to get this all straightened out with help from a lawyer. In the end, he was advised to contact the Israeli consulate if he was ever going to go to Israel, as he could be arrested after getting off the plane.

Later in my teens, while hanging out with my hippie friends at Morse Beach smoking pot, someone asked me to pass the doogee. I asked if they knew what "mondoo" meant, remembering the dogs of my childhood. I discovered that "mondoo" is a slang term for heroin, which I have never partaken of, and that "doogee" means marijuana, a favorite pastime of mine.

Young Dawn

4

Summoning Revolution

Mom, Dad, Amy, Dawn, Danny

Since the Beatles had appeared on Ed Sullivan, Amy and I had been all about the music. That evening in 1964, we'd sat on the green shag carpet on our living room floor, glued to the twenty-four-inch TV arguing about which Beatle we liked better. "She Loves You! Yeah, Yeah, Yeah, Oooooh!" Those cute mop-top heads shaking and singing mesmerized us. Amy loved Paul, and so did I. And then words appeared on the screen under John just as I shifted my attention to him. "Sorry, girls! He's married."

Was that a thing? You could grow up to marry someone in a rock band? My imagination went wild. This appealed to a new sensibility, a magnetism I didn't understand. I could dance my life away with that kind of man. I wanted to marry someone in a band!

Mother bought their records and played them so often on the living room stereo that Amy, Danny, and I soon knew all the words and would sing them while twisting our little tushes with The Beatles.

I recall one summer day at the beach in 1966. Mother appeared at the shoreline several yards from us holding our homemade terry-cloth ponchos in a print of oversized pink-and-green flowers with matching green cha-cha-ball trim. We knew what was coming next.

"Get out of the water! Your lips are turning blue," she bellowed.

Amy and I took our time splashing back to shore, where she bundled us in said ponchos, sending us to sit on the beach blanket. The sky overhead was hazy, filling with big, white clouds that gave a little relief from the heat. We plunked down in resignation but heard the sound of drums and cymbals and electric guitars very close in the distance. We looked up to see where it was coming from.

A small crowd had gathered on the cement barrier surrounding the grass-covered hill a block over near Morse beach. Amy and I instantly looked at each other and without a word were on our feet running, not looking back.

Mother yelled, "Where are you going?"

"Just there! Look!" I pointed while running toward the hippie rock band playing live music. A group of people crowded around to listen and dance.

The hill formed a stage for the band a few feet above the gathering crowd. We pushed our way through until we were in front. Those charismatic boys were adorned in tight, navel-baring, hip-rocking, blue-jean bell-bottoms. These were paired with suede, fringed vests, tight, sleeveless T-shirts—or no shirts at all—and bandana headbands holding their long locks from their eyes. I fell in love with this new look, begging my mother for bell-bottoms. I wanted to look that cool! Those young men with their long hair and raucous energy were seeds sprouting from that shag carpeting.

This experience had to be directly inhaled. At nine and ten, with our wet pigtails and animated ponchos swinging to the beat, no one stopped us. We were entranced, with huge smiles and dancing feet, the music feeding our souls like ice cream. At that moment I realized that live music energized me and made me happier than anything. The crowd swelled and swayed. Mother soon joined us. She couldn't resist the beat either. The music, hypnotizing as we continued to sway along, united all of us strangers. We had the beat in common, and that moment was all there was. We were strangers no more.

△ ▽ △ ▽

I had just turned eleven, and in the summer before sixth grade, we moved to our house in West Rogers Park, where I joined a gang of neighborhood misfits, including my cousin Dennis. We were not interested in being popular with the social climbers of the status quo or in joining any of the usual school activities. Instead, we listened to rock music, dressed like hippies, and entertained modern ideas of peace, equality, and feminism, while keeping up on current events like the Vietnam War. We dared each other to take on the world on our own terms. A nearby park became our clubhouse, and our meeting spot there a set of benches shaded by the enormous boughs of maple trees. We hung out at the park as long as the weather held, and at each other's homes when it didn't.

Earlier that summer, Mother had taken me to buy my first bra at Sears Roebuck. My clothes had all been showing obvious chest inflation. We browsed the racks as she kept handing me selections to try on. With my arms overflowing, we headed for the dressing room. I vividly recall the heavy curtains of the dressing room, fitting the straps over my shoulders and bending over to make sure my budding tits fell into the little cups of the bra. Then I would have to stand back up, maneuvering my hands—still holding both straps behind—while trying to hook the closures together evenly. This was quite a trick. My mother constantly chimed in with, "How does that one feel?" or, "Let me see!" This moment also marked the beginning of something I was hardly prepared to handle yet very excited to receive: attention from boys.

New School

Knowing it was getting late, I ran downstairs on the first day of sixth grade to find my mother, Danny, and Amy waiting for me. Mother looked at me with a worried frown. "You're wearing that? Never mind, there's no time to change. I'm walking you over to make sure you're in the same class as Dennis. And that way, Danny and Amy won't be too nervous."

At the principal's office, we were welcomed and given directions to our rooms. Mom escorted Danny to his. I bid them all farewell with glee and danced down the hallway and up the stairs in my flowered mini dress—as short as I dared—wanting to make an impression. Girls still had to wear dresses every day, and if I was going to have to bend to their rules, they were going to have to suffer my fashion sense. I wanted everyone to know that I could lead the way. I was the one who made things happen.

As I opened the door of the classroom, everything came to a standstill. My new classmates had gotten wind of this wild girl, Dennis' cousin, and anxiously awaited my entrance. My thick, dark, curly hair flowed freely down my shoulders and back, seeming to float all around me, my dress appearing little more than a long T-shirt.

Mrs. Queenie Golden stood stoutly at the front of the class sporting a wardrobe from the forties. Her long, silver locks were neatly pinned behind her head in a bun, which framed her soft, puffy, oval face. She gave me a long, steady look up and down, with a welcoming smile but a question in her eyes. I handed her the slip identifying her new student.

"Welcome to Rogers School, Dawn. Please take the empty desk in the back." She raised her arm and pointed her hand.

"My nickname is Didi. That's what everyone calls me. You can too."

"All right, class. We shall call her Didi."

I turned and strutted down the aisle, smiling at the gawking faces on the way to my seat. The girls sensed I possessed the power to lead them to change, while the boys knew they finally had a sexy, budding woman in their midst.

After school, our gang would go hang out under the tall maple tree. But the older kids in the neighborhood from high school hung out there too. Some had cars and would park across the street. When they were there, we had to move to the benches further into the park because they had seniority. The older boys always noticed me—or should I say they noticed the roundness of my chest. It was a funny thing, my change of figure bringing all this new attention. I wasn't a bad-looking girl: tall and long legged, with a glimpse of mischievousness in my eyes. But it was always my chest that fascinated the boys. I became curious about this emerging sexuality, about how it made me feel and how I was attracted to boys.

One of my favorite places to visit was my friend Brenda's house. Her mother was deaf, but she loved to feel the beat of music in the house. It didn't matter what kind. She would often sit next to the TV and rest her arm on it just to feel the vibration. Maybe that was why she didn't mind when her son, Michael, practiced with his band buddies in the basement. When they were there playing, you could hear it from the street—my signal to go over and check them out.

Brenda and I would creep down the stairs not to disturb them and sit at the bottom step, listening. This was so cool! I couldn't believe my luck: living just two doors down from this musical infusion! I would relive the feelings Amy and I experienced while dancing in front of that band at Morse beach, the music overwhelming us with joy as it pulsed through our veins.

Michael's bandmates were an unusual bunch. They were all nerds and did not share the good looks of Robert Plant or Jimi Hendrix. But they had long hair, dressed in the usual hippie garb of blue-jean bell-bottoms and T-shirts, and could carry a beat. On breaks, they would talk with us while smoking joints.

Michael introduced us to new and unusual music. "Have you ever heard of Frank Zappa?" he asked one day, queuing up an album on the basement stereo with a weird grin. Frank Zappa was his favorite and soon became one of mine. Later Michael and his bandmates would sing Zappa's lyrics to me: "Only thirteen and she knows how to nasty." They loved to tease me, but I knew they lusted over me. To this day I still can't wear brown shoes—or anything else brown for that matter—because of Zappa's song "Brown Shoes Don't Make It." It tackles the stereotypes and drudgery of modern life and its mundanity, and a husband that's cheating on his wife with his "teenage baby." After listening to a few tunes and passing joints, they would go back to their equipment and play some more.

This music was different from Morse beach for me. I was feeling it in a whole new way. The music churned my hormones into an uproar, spurning my later discovery that I loved sex and didn't think marriage was necessary.

5

Firsts

The world began to spin faster in the late sixties. Timothy Leary was teaching young people to "turn on, tune in, and drop out." I did my best at that and saw Hendrix, started smoking pot, and lost my virginity within the span of my thirteenth year.

"I like Marijuana, you like Marijuana, we like Marijuana too"

Craig was one of the older boys in high school with a car who hung out at the park sometimes. A nice-looking hippie with a full, thick head of long, sandy-blond hair, he was a loner, too cool to hang there all the time. One day, he pranced over to introduce himself with his blazing, sky-blue eyes and said, "Let's go for a walk." Flattered at the attention, I nodded. We strolled along the cement path through the park and exchanged all the usual chat. "Where do you live?" "What grade are you in?" "How old are you?"

Then he asked, "Do you want to get high?"

I hadn't done that yet and urgently responded, "Yes, I do. I've been wanting to for a while now, so this will be my first time."

He laughed and said, "You couldn't be with a better person."

We sat down on the grass far away from everyone else, obscured by the bushes. He pulled out a plastic baggie of pot and extended it under my nose. It held a powerful earthy and skunky odor, yet it wasn't unpleasant. He produced some rolling papers and arranged the bag on his lap to sit open while he rolled a joint over it to catch the crumbs. The process was fascinating. I paid very close attention to how he did it and asked when he was done, "Can I try to do that too?" Amused, he handed me the papers and bag and instructed me at each step. Mine came out too tight to smoke.

"There needs to be a little air in there for the smoke to ignite it," Craig offered helpfully. He lit up the one he had rolled, closed his eyes, and took a deep, long inhale before passing it to me. I tried to imitate his actions and immediately began hacking away, as any first-timer would.

Craig suppressed his giggles and said, "Try again! This time a little slower. Don't inhale so much. Then try to hold it in as long as you can." This time it went easier, and we passed the joint back and forth until my thoughts felt like they were floating away and everything struck me as funny.

"You must be getting thirsty. I am," Craig said as he got up. We walked down the path to the water fountain to quench our dry mouths, talking about the experience. I asked if it always felt this way, he told jokes, and the both of us laughed at the silliest little things.

Yes, I suppose smoking pot was my gateway drug, as I soon moved on to LSD, peyote, and mescaline. They all expanded my mind in a way nothing else ever could. I experienced as much as I could, as often as I could, searching for that something . . .

Hendrix

Brenda and I had bought tickets for Jimi Hendrix months in advance. It was our first big concert, and we were really stoked about going. On the big night—December 1, 1968—I put on my favorite purple corduroy bell bottoms and borrowed a blouse from my mother. It had wrist-length puffy sleeves featuring a long self-tie around the collar, giving it an Edwardian look.

Then Mother asked me," How are you getting there?" Hendrix was playing at The Coliseum just south of downtown.

"Um, we'll take the bus to the L and walk," I fibbed. Brenda and I were going to hitch.

"I don't like the idea of you wandering around in that neighborhood. I'll give you a ride," she returned.

My mother was right: that area of downtown was a bit seedy. Everything became grayer and grittier the further past downtown we rode. When we reached the Coliseum, Mother was about to drop us off when she noticed a line at the box office, meaning tickets were still available. After we got out of the car, she said, "I'll see you inside. Maybe I can still get a ticket and drive you home too."

This was going to be weird. Here we were all ready to be on our own, and now we were chaperoned! But we were there and about to see Jimi Hendrix! Hopefully, we could get lost in the crowd.

Brenda led the way, and we sped through the place as fast as we could, escaping my mother's gaze. Our seats were off to the side of the stage and two big sections down. Who knew in those days about picking the seats you wanted? We were just happy to have the tickets. The opening band was lackluster, but we suffered through them, not wanting to venture from our seats in case we ran into my mother.

Finally, Jimi took the stage in all his splendor: purple satin bell-bottoms, a tie-dyed shirt open to his waist, and a scarf wrapped around his forehead to keep his afro from his eyes. He was one sexy dude. His playing immediately jolted the room with the fire of his guitar, and he played non-stop with ease. At one point he lifted the guitar over his head, plucking its strings behind his back! Then he brought it back to his face and played using his teeth, all without missing a beat and with a look of reverence on his face as if in some kind of holy trance. This is still the most amazing show I have witnessed.

The music hypnotized us. It was like an induced high—not that the audience wasn't beforehand. Joints were being passed freely around the rows whether you knew someone or not. Everybody must get stoned!

After the show, we found my mom out front waiting for us.

"What did you think? Did you like the show?" I asked.

"You're not going to believe this, but I was able to get a seat in the tenth-row center. It was a terrific view. I could see his navel!" Did my mother seem a little high?! No, she would never do that!

We listened to FM on the car radio all the way home, high on the spirit of Hendrix.

Cherryville

One day Brenda announced she had a boyfriend and asked me to visit him with her, so we hitched over to his small, one-room studio apartment just off busy Clark Street in East Rogers Park.

When we arrived, I discovered that he was more of a freak than a hippie—as in the kind you would meet at a traveling sideshow—and he was much older than we were. In fact, he'd been to Viet Nam and had been discharged for injury. His room contained a bed, a side table with a radio, a hot plate, and a coffee maker. There was no decoration or anything to give it character. I felt stifled by the starkness and his apparent attraction to me.

He and Brenda sat down on the bed, inviting me to do the same. There was nowhere else to sit. Then she pulled out a joint and lit it up, and we passed it around (I was an old pro now!). Her boyfriend turned the radio on while he moved closer to me, telling me how pretty I was and stroking my hair before moving his hands down to my chest.

Brenda had already lost her cherry to him, and I didn't sense her minding that he was coming on to me. I don't know why I didn't resist him. I did feel a little like a deer in the headlights. He asked if I had ever had sex before, but I couldn't speak, mesmerized under his spell.

His long, stringy, blond hair, pulled back with a bandana, revealed a sinister, contorted face somewhat like an ogre. But for a man with no physical appeal, he was very sure of himself as he proceeded to dominate me. His hands were all over me, exploring in my pants, and suddenly a finger went up inside, and he said with an excited expression on his garish face, "Well, looky here! A virgin after all."

He continued to undress me, and I just let him, cringing at each new place he would touch that excited yet mortified me at the same time. I didn't want to lose my virginity to this ogre or in this way, but I was too baffled to stop him.

When he was finished, I found blood on the sheet and went to the bathroom to cry and clean myself of his lingering presence. Returning to the main room, I looked at Brenda and urged, "We have to go."

He laughed and thanked Brenda for bringing me over. I would never go there again. Brenda and I never spoke of it again—not even to this day!

Today it's called rape. Back then, it was just what happened, and one dealt with it. It was the time of free love. But I felt complicit: I let it happen. I went through the motions feeling like I could handle it—after all, Brenda was able to. Unfortunately, I didn't understand that what he was really doing was a crime. It is very disturbing for me to look back at this today. I can't even remember his name and feel like such an idiot for allowing it to happen. This could never happen again! I needed to find real love, someone who appreciated me, someone to feel right about indulging my raging hormones with.

6

Sex & Drugs & Rock'n'Roll Summer of 1970

When I was eight, that curly redhead on the playground was just too hot to handle.

"No, stay away from him!" Aunt Jackie warned. "He's a bad boy." She was friends with his mother; she knew. Nonetheless, the excitement was attractive. I knew I had to stay away, that he would be trouble with a capital T. But how did it feel to kiss a boy? I had to have the taste on my lips. So I found Jeff, with his dark Beatles mop top. We were all of nine, and I got my kiss. It wasn't enough, though. There must be more! Something that makes you want to melt into another. I watched, I waited, and I began growing into my body, which began outgrowing me and turning into a woman. The hormone tap had cranked on, and I couldn't help myself. Little boys would not do. I had to find a man.

After a few rough starts, the boys all thought that because I had the equipment, I would play the game. That's all they wanted to do: play. What I didn't realize was that it was all I wanted to do too—just not with them. There had to be more—for instance, those men with long hair, hanging in the parks and beaches, carrying protest signs, smoking weed, and tripping on acid. I had to play with them. I had to take in what they were. I had to grow up into this woman's body quickly because the tap was boiling over and needed a place to flow.

It was a time of free love. No one judged you, and there were many one-nighters. We all danced and changed partners.

I met my first older hippie boyfriend Jim Moore in Lincoln Park in the late summer of my fourteenth year, our eyes magnetically connecting. He was tall and thin with long, thick brown hair hanging to the middle of his back, a handlebar mustache, and generous sideburns. Furriness poked out from under his shirt and up and down his arms like a teddy bear.

With a slow measured gait, he approached me and asked, "What's your name? I'm Jim." His easy smile and sweet blue eyes showed me a kind-hearted man.

I stuttered a little and started to say Didi, but instead replied, "Dawn. Well, Didi is a nickname, but Dawn is my real name. Please call me Dawn."

Smiling broadly in return, he said, "Okay, Dawn," and sat down on the grass beside me. My heart began to melt as we talked about all kinds of hippie stuff.

Soon, we were dating, going to concerts and parties, and meeting up at Lincoln Park. He lived with the Melrose Bros in a communal house, a nineteenth-century building painted bright blue with white trim and bits of gingerbread woodwork around the windows and big front porch. The house was filled with antique furniture bought at thrift stores and the sweet smell of herb being smoked within. Jim had an ancient four-poster bed that engulfed his tiny room, and the living room was filled with old wooden side tables, a glass-fronted hutch, and big, overstuffed velvet chairs and couches from the forties that made it cozy to sit by the fire. It was shabby chic before the trend.

I thought it was so cool that the Melrose Bros and their girlfriends all got along so well—or seemed to. They cooked vegetarian meals, had heated meetings, and all got high together. I felt like a sponge, an observer of all the new ideas there. I wanted to learn everything about how to be a grownup and live communally. But Jim broke my heart on Valentine's Day! It was so hard, but I had to learn to move on.

This was also a time of experimentation for me. I can't tally how many drugs I took. LSD, mescaline, peyote, mushrooms, pot, and cocaine—they were the highs I enjoyed because they were mostly derived from plants and uplifted me while giving me insight. Downers, on the other hand, I didn't like at all. I avoided alcohol and have never taken heroin. Incoherence never appealed to me. And speed was always a bit too much because I already bore a boundless amount of energy and it made me feel edgy. But coke was different. In those days, it was real cocaine—more of an opiatic experience and not so speedy. It gave you the feeling you could do anything.

LSD turned out to be a trip and a half. I had been hanging out with a group of guys I'd met at Morse beach after Jim when I was fourteen. They were in their late teens and early twenties and were "bad boy" hippies, so of course, I was attracted to them.

One summer day in 1970, we were at a big concert at Soldier Field downtown, where The Who was headlining. My latest boyfriend, Artie, was selling some acid called Grey Thunder, and I decided it was time to have my first experience. Artie handed me a tab with a big smile on his face saying, "It will be fun, I'll watch out after you."

In those days, if you had a ticket stub, they let you go in and out of the stadium all day, so I left the concert with him and a couple of the guys to pick up a few others in their red Chevy convertible with the top down. The sun was high and blazing.

Their apartment was in a hillbilly neighborhood with scrappy front yards and hardly a tree or anything green in sight. When we approached, the acid was just starting to kick in, so I was questioning what was going on, wondering if it was real or not. But it seemed that several cop cars were parked in front of my friends' building, blue bubbles flashing. Handcuffed to the chain-link fence in front were several of our pals, heads downcast. We drove by, and a hillbilly neighbor with a buzz cut yelled out, "Hey, there's some more of them hippies! Go get 'em!"

A squad car stopped us before we turned the corner. It was like the keystone cops descending on us as they yelled at us to get out and began ripping the car apart. The scene was surreal; everything was in blazing color like a cartoon and seemed electrified. I stood behind the car just staring at the commotion as if I wasn't a part of it—just an observer whose body happened to be there. Then one of the cops looked up with a smile as he took a pill container from the gas tank filler behind the license plate. He rattled the bottle and said, "You are all coming with us."

I instantly recognized it: the prescription pill container filled with Grey Thunder.

At the station, I was seated next to Artie in a small, drab, gray room with six of our friends squeezed together on a bench around a table. The cops were in the process of assigning charges. They looked at Artie, who was holding my hand, and said to him, "How about contributing to the delinquency?" Artie and I slowly unclasped our hands.

"Young lady, you are going to have to come with us." They led me into another room with a desk and a few chairs. Two cops sat there: the good one and the bad one. They spoke as if I wasn't there.

"What do you think? Is she high?" asked Bad Cop.

Good Cop replied, "Nah, I think she's just scared."

I looked at Good Cop, slowly nodding "yes," but didn't speak.

Their hands were full with my friends, and they just wanted to be rid of me, so they phoned my parents. However, no one was home, so they called my Aunt Blanche, who sent Uncle Rolly down to get me. A TV producer for both the "Dick Tracy Show" and "International Marketplace," a Chicago folk-music show, Uncle Rolly liked to drink and had an infectious smile. I was so glad Aunt Blanche didn't come herself. I'd have never heard the end of it!

My uncle arrived looking like he'd just left the couch, in his loafers with no socks, chinos, and a white T-shirt with the sleeves rolled up. After a few words with him, they released me, and as we were walking out of the station, Uncle Rolly looked at my dirty bare feet and asked, "Where are your shoes?"

"We were at a concert in Soldier Field, and I left them there," I replied sheepishly.

"Let's go back and get them."

Uncle Rolly and I got into his red Cadillac convertible, and since it was a nice day for a drive, he decided to take the top down. I was so high that it was hard to have a conversation! The air was thickly filled with psychedelic patterns only I could see, and it all left me fairly speechless. I didn't know what to expect on my first acid trip, so I just kept my mouth shut. But I did manage to chirp, "Thank you for picking me up. I'm so sorry for causing all this trouble. It must be quite a burden for you with Steven and me being in so much trouble."

His son had recently been busted for selling pot in college, but he just waved it off. He was much more interested in the pleasant ride down Lake Shore Drive with the top down, a cigarette dangling from the corner of his mouth, his salt-and-pepper pompadour blowing in the breeze.

I still remember the words of the song flowing from the radio: "Spill the wine, take that pearl." But in those days, I thought Eric

Burdon was singing, "Spill the wine, dig that girl." No matter, the song was like an acid trip and epitomized the one I was on.

When we arrived at Soldier Field, I ran in and miraculously found the blanket on the grass with my neon-yellow Keds in the middle of the crowded concert. I wished for a moment that I could stay and watch The Who as they played but thought I shouldn't let Uncle Rolly wait too long. I was in enough trouble!

Getting grounded didn't really mean much. Yeah, my parents would explode and say, "You can't go anywhere! You can't do anything!" In the end, though, they would have to stay home with me, which Dad was certainly never going to do and Mom had no patience for. So it went like this: a few days at home, then friends called and came over, and soon, the whole thing just faded, and out the door I'd be.

My siblings and I had an unusual upbringing. Our parents trusted us and did their best to let us know that telling the truth was always the way to go. Though many times I did lie, it was mainly by omission. When my parents would ask, "Where were you?" I'd reply, "Out with friends," or "Morse Beach." This was likely true, but no further details were given, and Mom and Dad never really checked on us. Life was no longer about them. I was growing into whom I thought I was. Smoking marijuana and ingesting psychedelics opened up a whole new world for me, one in which I was constantly seeking out other truths. I would see little inklings of things that interested me, adopt them, and move on. I loved making my own clothes. I would find India-print bedspreads that were perfect to sew into sexy blouses, skirts, and loose pants. And I listened to all kinds of rock music, saw as many live concerts as possible, and read books like *Be Here Now* by Ram Dass and *Living on the Earth* by Alicia Bay Laurel. Nothing seemed to be completely taking hold of me except what revolved around music and the urgings of my hormones.

A couple of months after that first acid trip, my mother found an old jewelry box in my room filled with ten, nicely rolled joints. It had never occurred to me that she would search through my stuff.

"Come up here," she called when I came home from school.

None the wiser, I climbed the staircase and followed her into the bathroom. She reached up to a tall shelf and displayed the box she'd found.

"What do we have here," she sarcastically spat.

When I laughed in response, she said, "This is no laughing matter. I've been too lenient with you, and it's time to take action."

"What do you mean?" I asked. "You have those little ceramic pipes on your dresser, and I know what the residue looks and smells like. You've been smoking too," I smirked.

"That's not the point. I'm your mother. It's time to set some boundaries." She walked over to the toilet, lifted the lid, and upturned the joints into the water as she flushed them down.

"What did you do that for?" I shrieked.

"Because you need to learn some discipline. You can't do anything you want. I'm laying down the rules. I will allow you to smoke, but only at home where I can see who you're with."

Okay, so this wasn't so bad. Mom knew she couldn't keep me at home, but she was trying the best she could. And she was not banning me from smoking altogether. But she'd just flushed my stash, and I was pissed off!

"And I have more news for you," she said.

Okay, so what else? I thought. I looked up at her with vague disinterest.

"Your father smokes it too!"

Now, this *was* news. "You're kidding me! How can that be?" I exclaimed.

"He found out I was smoking, so he asked to try it. Now we get together with our friends and smoke."

You could have knocked me over with a feather.

This was the beginning of a very strange era in our family life. One early evening I came home to find my parents and a few of their friends hanging out in front of the living room fireplace, passing joints.

"Come in and join us," my Aunt Adrienne said, holding out a joint to me.

"Um, okay," I said, feeling a little flustered and taken by surprise—not realizing I should have said, "No, thanks."

My aunt asked, "What do you think about us all smoking pot together?"

"Uh, cool," I said, as I took the joint from her. I couldn't express how I really felt, which was really uncomfortable.

My parents were acting like my friends, and it didn't feel right. It was too unfamiliar and certainly unexpected. Seeing my authority figures act the way my friends did made me want to bottle my feelings up.

I told them, "I'm tired and going up to my room. Thanks for the hit."

Grant Park Riot

In July of 1970, Brenda and I hitchhiked to Grant Park to see Sly and the Family Stone in concert. It was billed as a huge, free event, and we weren't going to miss it for anything. We also thought it would be fun to take some acid and popped some along the way. Mom decided she had to go too and took my sister Amy, but they were coming later, so we arranged to meet them. Mom even brought her camera to document the show, as photography had become her new hobby.

The crowd was enormous, but Grant Park could accommodate. Most of the people were clustered near the bandshell, with its original shell-shaped backdrop, and spreading out behind them a few blocks towards the Field Museum was a large, grassy expanse. Brenda and I combed the benches in front—no seats available—and kept looking for a place to roost until the time we planned to meet up with my mother and Amy at Buckingham Fountain behind the bandshell. The crowd was split pretty evenly between black and white, with lots of hippies in either case, and cops parked on the grass by the sides ready for trouble.

We found Mom and Amy just as the acid was beginning to stir and wandered the crowd trying to watch the opening bands. It was a good distraction for my mother that kept her from paying too much attention to us. Then we began to hear rumors in the crowd that Sly might not show, and people started to get testy. They didn't want to hear the other bands and began shouting at the stage. My mother thought we should get out of the way; she could feel the mounting tension and sensed it was going to erupt. So we walked to the back of the field.

Brenda and I looked at each other, not speaking but knowing what the other was feeling as our vision turned hallucinogenic. The field looked like an oblong bowl extending out from the bandshell stage, its edges rising up to the main park level lined with bushes and flower gardens. Now it seemed like a stage set for drama, with the crowd moving, arms waving wildly. The aura was changing from good natured to aggressive.

Brenda, Amy, and I sat down in the grass on the upper rim, far away from the shell in front of the bushes. We had a good view of the action from there, but my mother decided to venture into the crowd to get some photos.

The acid was raging now, and I asked Brenda, "Does it look like it's all turning into a giant cartoon?" She nodded in agreement, and we watched the unfolding scene in astonishment. People were running everywhere, clustering around the cop cars, flipping them over, and then lighting them on fire. Others were throwing things at the stage, while the rest just ran to get out of the way.

Amy asked, "Where did Mother go?"

"Into the crowd to take pictures, but I've lost track of her," I answered.

None of us wanted to go into the crowd to find her, so I said, "She can take care of herself."

Amy went bitchy and said, "I really need some aspirin, and I have to get out of here. I'm going up to the street to ask people in cars for some." There, traffic had come to a standstill on Balboa Drive behind us by the lake.

I said, "We'd better stick together in this mayhem so no one else gets lost."

As soon as we started asking people, it was apparent that we really needed to just go home. Bodies were dashing from the bushes and running between the cars on Balboa to escape the riot on the field. Once we found Amy her aspirin, we started asking for rides and finally found someone who would take us all the way back to Rogers Park. As we got into the back seat of that car, I took a deep breath, feeling a sense of relief to be sheltered from the mayhem.

Mother made it home later and was very happy that we were back safe and sound. She had had an inner sense that I would get Amy and Brenda out safely. But in fact, she had barely gotten out herself, driving around frantically for a while, watching the burning cars, and worrying about where we could be—although she did come home with a few rolls of fantastic photos of the melee.

Later that fall while high on acid at a party, I mistakenly smoked a joint sprinkled with angel dust. There I sat, watching the air turn into giant, exaggerated, vibrating colors, the smoke turning into little paisleys floating around the partygoers. My body felt like cement (angel dust is a horse tranquilizer), but my mind was acutely alert. I began thinking about how these LSD experiences were becoming challenging when a tall man strode into the room trailing beautiful, long, sandy-blond hair, a whoosh of paisleys in his wake. His big moustache lifted as he grinned, and a rainbow-knit Robin Hood cap topped his flowing locks. His presence reminded me of a giant elf; there was an air of magic about him.

I asked a friend sitting next to me, "Who is that guy?"

He laughed and said, "Oh, that's Captain Teeth."

Captain Teeth's eyes landed on mine. He stepped closer, knelt down, handed me a feather and a lit piece of incense, and said, "Hi, my name is James. I want to be your friend." His smile showed where he had gotten his nickname: two oversized, rabbit-like front teeth extended from his top lip.

James glided down next to me as my friend got up, and as we talked through the night, he stayed close. He had been traveling and was brimming with information about natural health and vegetarianism, and he explained that he understood how it felt when the high got away from you.

I could not have caught the L home on my own, so James took me to his place that night, deciding to watch over my fragile state of mind. His father was out of town, and James was staying at his high-rise apartment by the lake. There, he shared stories of going to Tennessee to Steve Gaskins' farm and visiting California, where people were living communally, growing their own food, and making their own clothes. We saw each other off and on from there, going to concerts and parties and, of course, having lots of good sex.

Once, he took me to a tiny health-food store that reminded me of an old-fashioned general store. The wooden shelves behind the counters were piled with bags of items and crates lined the walls filled with produce and barrels of bulk grains, rice, and beans that you could scoop yourself and then have weighed. James showed me the best foods to buy and introduced me to Dr. Bronner's peppermint soap, which is still a staple of mine. I learned so much about healthy eating, with James preparing our meals and showing me how to combine foods.

Many of our friends were into the Grateful Dead, and James and I saw their concerts whenever they were in town. The Dead's sound guy, Sparky Razine, hailed from Chicago, and his cousin, Michael "Numbnuts" Stewart, was my friend Jeanie's boyfriend. One night, we visited the backstage area, which was separated from the audience by curtains attached to wheeled metal frames. There Sparky stood between a pair of them, smiling as he dispensed LSD from an eyedropper into our plastic cups while we all lined up. Dancing our way back to the front of the stage, we twirled the night away on this mass trip together. It was like a religious experience; everyone was smiling and feeling so high and one with the music. Later, Sparky showed up onstage with a bucket filled with joints and handed them to the musicians, who then tossed them out to the audience. It was always about sex and drugs and rock and roll. Ever the cliché, yet ever the truth.

Then one day, James announced, "I just wanted to let you know I'm moving back to California in a few days."

"Wow, that's kind of sudden," I said. "Why?"

He replied, "You'll just have to come out and see for yourself. That's where it's all happening!"

I didn't feel like I had to question him further. My heart was a bit more tempered by then and wasn't too trampled after his departure, but his words left a deep impression.

Several months after James departed, his friend Roy rolled into town in a panel van lined with a patchwork of multi-colored carpets: a home on wheels. It was amazing how he fitted out the van to be so cozy. It had a little kitchen, a sitting area, and a sleeping loft. Originally from Chicago, Roy had just driven in from LA to visit his ill mother.

He always seemed very sure of himself, with an air of mystery behind his shoulder-length curly brown hair and goatee. He wore a thick, oat-colored Mexican sweater jacket, a wide band of contrasting dark Aztec designs circling the middle, and white cotton pants. His dark eyes penetrated deep into my soul. I developed the biggest crush on him, and the feeling was mutual, so we began a saucy little affair.

Roy appreciated how I expressed my creative spirit with the clothes I made. He mentioned working as a cook in a restaurant but would never speak about LA. Instead, we'd discuss the latest bands and vegetarianism, and smoke herb. As he was only in Chicago for a couple of weeks, we made the most of it. We would make sweet love, then sleep in that loft bed in his patchwork cave.

And then he was gone.

7

The Last Gasps of Domesticity

My school grades were suffering from cutting classes, hanging out with friends in Newtown, and getting stoned. I just wanted to escape from it all.

After seeing my report card one day, my father asked me, "What's going on with you? I know you can't be failing in everything, and you leave every day for school. But your attendance record is terrible!"

"School really doesn't interest me, anymore," I sighed while staring at the floor.

Dad asked, "Why?"

This was surprising. He was not trying to fight with me but rather to understand.

"There's nothing I want to learn there," I told him.

He asked, "What do you want to learn?"

"I want to learn about things more relevant to my life, not just math, geography, and science. I'm looking for deeper answers about belief, fairness, health, and a natural lifestyle. I heard about an experimental school called Metro. They call it a school without walls. Its headquarters is downtown. Everyone checks in daily and then goes out to classes stationed at museums, offices, and locations all over the city."

"What if I could get you into Metro? I have a friend with connections to the Board of Education."

"That would be great," I answered in surprise.

In a month or so, I was riding the L downtown in the morning, ready for a new adventure in learning. I'd spent a year and a half at Sullivan High School and would finish out my sophomore year at Metro. While there, I signed up for classes in bird study at a park, Silva Mind Control (a self-help and meditation program developed by José Silva) in an office building, yoga at a studio in Lincoln Park, and vegetarianism at a restaurant called Ratso's. I would receive credit for physical education when I rode my bike downtown.

I loved the freedom of roaming all over the city and met a whole new group of friends. We would panhandle on State Street for extra cash and hang out on the Art Institute's stairs, where all the hippies met downtown. Plus, there were convenient gardens in the park behind it where we could get high.

Going downtown every day was invigorating. I would walk down State Street and investigate all the shop windows—especially the ones farther south and on the side streets that catered to the black community. Their clothes were so colorful, stylish, and loud, and their shoes and accessories all had incredible style.

My mother was expanding her mind too and soon found herself wanting to go out and make some money of her own so she could be a little more independent. She found a job in a cafe on Rush Street called Melvin's. But she was craving a bigger change in her life. Frustrated with her relationship with my father, she met a man named Bill and began an affair. My father found out, blew his top, and filed for divorce, and Mother moved in with Bill.

At the same time, my sister, Amy, met a guy named Jay, who played guitar in a band called Flight. She was only thirteen, and Jay was nineteen, but he still lived at home not far from us. When his parents found out about him and Amy, they threw him out. Trying to hold our rocking ship from sinking, my father suggested Jay sleep in our den on the pull-out couch. Of course, I was out getting high all the time, so I wasn't really paying attention to what was happening at home. None of it bothered me; I was much more interested in my new life.

△ ▽ △ ∀

Dad hired a cutthroat divorce lawyer who advised him to do some nasty stuff for his defense. A few weeks before the court date, my father showed up at school to take me to a doctor.

"Why?" I asked him. "I'm confused. No one told me about any doctor's appointment."

"It's just a general check-up. Mother can't take you, so I am." My father seemed as if it was nothing out of the ordinary.

When we arrived at the doctor's office, it wasn't my usual physician. Dad never said another word about it.

Eventually, it all came out. After the trial, my mother told me the whole sad tale, sobbing.

"Your father arrived in court with a two-inch ball of hash in a glass jar, stating it was mine. The stash was both of ours."

I knew which one it was. I used to steal little bits from it.

"Then he presented an affidavit from that doctor you saw swearing you were no longer in possession of your virginity. It was enough to destroy my case, and now your father has the house and full custody of you, Amy, and Danny."

Soon after the divorce, my mother and Bill broke up. He wanted to return to his pregnant wife. Not able to face the fact that she'd lost the man she'd given up her family for, she decided to move to Colorado, where she could do something she loved: ski. She found a roommate and a little apartment in Aspen and got a job in a bar. That took her through the next ski season and some life experience she was robbed of when Dick got her pregnant at eighteen. She could ski in the daytime and hang out with The Eagles, a band in its infancy, at the bar at night!

In the meantime, Dick found himself a girlfriend, a blond giantess, and he brought her home to introduce us all. Madeline was very pretty and nice enough but really hard to relate to. It was awkward; she was not my mom, and I wasn't going to confide anything to her. How could my dad think we would just accept her so fast? So I steered clear of Dad and Madeline and went my own way. I continued to hang out downtown and failed miserably in most of my classes, except for yoga, vegetarianism, and bicycle riding. More and more, I'd escape to get high, no longer even bothering to make excuses.

My father wouldn't even bother to ask where I'd been. "So you're home?"

I'd answer simply, "Yeah."

Dad's treatment of Mom during the trial had put a dent in my respect for him. He had done everything he could to destroy her, which still smolders in a tiny, dark corner of my heart. And now, his relationship with Madeline was creating a bigger disconnect between us. At this point, I was running wild and failing in school, and Amy had moved her boyfriend, Jay, into her bedroom along with his dog, Smokey. Then there was poor Danny, who desperately needed his mother because Madeline couldn't possibly replace her.

Meanwhile, in Aspen, Mother was in despair, missing her children desperately. Eventually, her heart pulled her home. My father was happy to make it work again; his hands were tied. He came to the realization that we would never listen to him, rendering him powerless as a parent. Their divorce lasted fifteen months. They'd discovered they were both ready to deal with the devil they knew. Dad promptly dumped Madeline, and Audrey returned just before my sixteenth birthday in April.

She threw me a wonderful birthday party, shopping at Adam's Apple head shop to decorate the party, and bought hippie paraphernalia of peace patches, incense, and beaded necklaces to distribute as favors. She knew how to get our attention and make us happy, inviting my neighborhood friends and attempting to ground my perspective so that things would seem more normal. But it was not enough. I was growing restless. All of the turning on, tuning in, and dropping out had left a huge gap in my motivation. School bored me to blazes, and I was not interested in doing anything other than getting high, going to concerts, and having sex with handsome, older longhairs. And it all left me feeling empty. Wasn't there more to life than this? Everything I had been through with my parents' divorce, reconciliation, school, and broken hearts had only made me feel more lost. Wasn't I supposed to be finding enlightenment somewhere?

8

The Conjuring

By the end of June 1972, I was grateful school was out. I was again disillusioned with it, not learning anything useful, yearning for more. However, a significant summer was waiting in the wings. Some friends were planning a trip to Colorado for the Fourth of July and the first-ever Rainbow Gathering in Granby Pass.

All the hippie tribes had been invited, including the Hog Farm, Steve Gaskin's Farm, and anyone who wanted to be part of the newly forming Rainbow Tribe. I had to go—maybe the next step I was looking for would be there. It was a time when large music festivals were becoming popular, and they were few and far between. I had missed them all up to this point under the guise of "You're too young." Now I felt old enough. I found a job working at the Little King sandwich shop to save some cash and secured my place in an old, blue panel van with my pals.

After begging my parents for weeks to let me go, my mother eventually saw there was no holding me back. Even though she had only been home a short time, she agreed to let me follow my dreams. In fact, I had been planning to head toward the West Coast in the back of my mind for a while. Brenda and I used to dream of buying a Volkswagen van and driving out to California. An overwhelming impulse was pulling me to be there now.

Jeanie was a couple of years older than me. We had made friends going to Grateful Dead shows and had much in common, sewing our own clothes and supplementing our wardrobes with old thrift-shop finds. So we decided to be traveling companions. Gary was our driver, and a few assorted other friends piled in the van too. It was pretty close in there, with all our packs and supplies. And there was no air conditioning either, so it all became a little earthy smelling. There was a platform in the back with a mattress and storage underneath, a carpet on the floor with pillows to sit on, and only one other seat next to the driver. We filled the journey singing songs, smoking weed, having fun at rest stops to stretch our legs and snack, and napping on the long drive to Colorado. We arrived in the late afternoon at the Rainbow Gathering parking grounds after two days of traveling.

Jeanie and I climbed out of the van to find thousands of cars parked in a big open meadow at the base of a steep hill that led up to a plateau. It was hot, dry, and dusty, but the setting sun would soon cool things down. The festival was being held at the top of that hill, and we set out to hike it before the sun got too low. In many spots, we had to climb the trail like a ladder, using the rocks and tree roots mounded on top of each other like rungs. The path was also sketchy and hard to follow and took forever to traverse. Darkness shadowed us, and we were not prepared for it, but luckily the trail was teeming with many other hikers who were happy to assist.

When you're young, you're invincible, and somehow, we fumbled our way up that hill in the dark, laden with backpacks, finding our other friends to camp with. I look back and marvel at what an impulsive, oblivious fool I was. If I had not been so cute, gullible, and sweet, people would have never put up with me.

We awoke the next morning to a different world. Our camp of various tents was set up in a twenty-foot open space near the forest edge with a fire pit in the middle of it and a few tree stumps to sit on scattered around it. Hippies were *everywhere*, playing music, getting high, making breakfast, making love, being naked, dancing, playing, and spreading love and joy with everyone they met.

The rising sun warmed our souls as it climbed above the trees. The air felt crisp and clean, smelling of sweet pine, and it warmed further as the sun grew higher. Jeanie and I decided to go for a walk and take it all in. We were not alone; the path we followed was filled with a constant stream in both directions of souls with the same notion. I wanted to get in the mood, so I grabbed the edge of my T-shirt and yanked it over my head. Jeanie followed my lead. It felt so free not to wear a shirt—a privilege only men had. We both smiled broadly and looked at each other with a giggle, following the trail that connected all the campgrounds at the rim of the forest in what seemed like a big circle. The hippy guys all marveled at our freedom, and I think we inspired a few other gals to let it all hang out, as well. It soon felt very natural and I didn't even have another thought about the fact that I was a vulnerable teen prancing around half-naked in front of all these strangers.

The Hog Farm's communal kitchen offered a free breakfast. All we had to do was help out washing dishes. Atop long tables made of plywood on sawhorses were gigantic pots filled with steaming oatmeal. Wooden platters were piled high with slices of toast next to piles of paper plates and plastic utensils. The folks making all this happen were joyful in their work, greeting us with welcoming smiles. Long tree trunks on the forest floor served as seating. It felt good to eat a filling, warm meal and be treated like we belonged. After our meal, we wandered out to the meadows and fields to discover more of the land. People were gathered in little and big groups everywhere we looked. At one point, I saw a young man with flaming red hair serenading a large circle of folks. He sang songs of peace and love filled with sincerity, his guitar underpinning his songs with urgency.

The Rainbow Gathering had been inspired by the prophecy of the return of White Buffalo Woman, a wise and magical entity predicted by the Lakota to reunite all of Mother Earth's children with her powers. It was also supposed to signify the start of the Age of Aquarius. This Gathering continues to be held every Fourth of July somewhere in America, but the Rainbow Tribe is having a harder time finding places where their activities will be tolerated.

For three days, we got high, listened to music, had sex, heard a lot of storytelling, and met people from all over the country with a myriad of beliefs. It was all so intriguing, but too soon, it was over. Descending back down the hill proved to be much quicker than going up—not to mention easier in daylight. But Jeanie and I still took our time. We didn't want it to end and were basking in the afterglow of the gathering and sharing all our high points. At the bottom, we saw a group of people surrounding the old, blue van as we approached. Jeanie's sister Mary was there with her boyfriend, whose old Volvo was parked next to it. Everyone was rehashing their experience and what they were doing next. Gary, our driver, had to get back to Chicago for work, but Mary asked Jeanie if she wanted to go with them to Oregon. When I heard that they had room for one more, I jumped at the opportunity and threw my backpack in their trunk.

Dawn Hurwitz

Travelers to Rainbow Gathering. I'm second from top on right.

We had a fun drive across the northern states, stopping to rock hunt and fruitlessly searching for dinosaur bones. I spent a lot of the ride thinking about what was to come for me. Would I go to San Francisco to find a school or head down to LA to find James and Roy? When we arrived at the border of Oregon and California, I knew it was time to part ways.

"Thank you, folks, for the ride! This is where you can drop me off," I proclaimed with excitement.

Jeanie bore a face of disappointment. "You could come with us to Eugene. I hear there's a very cool community there that's doing good things," Jeanie begged.

"I'm sorry, Jeanie. But something has been pulling me to California for a long time. I have to find out what that is," I softly answered.

"Okay. I hope you find what you're looking for, but keep Eugene in mind if you don't," Jeanie sadly replied.

They left me at the roadside with big hugs and well wishes. Then I pulled my green frame backpack from the trunk, slung it on my back, and stuck out my thumb at Klamath Falls.

Me, appreciating the wonders of nature.

It didn't take long until a rusty, tan, sixties sedan with three hippie boys stopped to offer me a ride. They were on their way to San Francisco—a good first stop. My old friend Ducky lived there, and I knew I could stay with him for a bit. A coke dealer from Chicago, he had always been very kind toward me—especially if he thought sex might be involved.

The drive through the redwoods on the way was magnificent, and the boys had some great weed and some good radio stations blasting from the speakers to make the ride pleasant. It was a hot summer day, but the wind from the open windows brought a pleasant, woody-scented breeze. I sat in the back seat with the one who seemed to be their guiding light. He gave directions, tossing his thick, blond curls from his eyes as he searched the map. He was kind of cute, but very loud and aggressive. Everyone wanted to stop in the redwoods; it was impossible not to want to get out and worship those trees. We drove right through a really huge one that had been hollowed out underneath and found a place to park.

Trails trickled out in several directions as we split up, our feet taking us deeper into the forest. I wasn't interested in the blond boy, but he was zoning in on me. I tried to be self-contained, but he grabbed my hand and tried to pull me close. Out in the middle of a forest with strangers, I wasn't sure what to do next.

I mustered, "I need a bathroom," and pulled away, hurrying back down the path. We waited at a restroom near the parking lot, met the other boys, and continued on our way.

The joints kept being passed around in the car, and the blond boy kept scooting closer to me in the back seat. I would try to compose myself, scooting a few inches away. I didn't feel scared, but rather cornered and uneasy, so I decided it was easier to just do as he wanted than to fight it. It might have been dangerous otherwise, and I would get scared. This way was just easier. He didn't seem violent, just filled with testosterone, and I had certainly settled for worse than him, but this was getting old. I didn't like being a victim. Pulling my legs over his lap, he moved his hands down my loose, India-print pants.

△ ▽ △ ▽

When signs said San Francisco was getting closer, I got out my map trying to locate Ducky's address. This also distracted Blond Curls from wanting to get further with me. He tried to interest me in going with them, but no dice! They found Ducky's place in a sweet neighborhood of low, two-flat houses and apartments and left me on his doorstep a little shaken but safe, determined, and still whole.

I discovered that Ducky was now an artist creating stained glass lamps and doing well selling them. It was fascinating to watch how he would arrange all the pieces on paper and then construct them over an upturned colander.

Ducky asked, "What are your plans while you're here?"

I said, "Do you remember the Metro High School in Chicago?"

"Yes."

"I've been going there, but it's turned into a dead end for me. I fell in with a crowd that was going nowhere fast. They just get high all day and hang out at the Art Institute. I was hoping to find another alternative school here and heard of one in the Haight."

Ducky answered," Be careful. Things have become pretty degraded in the city. But you should go and check it out. You're welcome to stay here during your search."

Somehow, I knew my destiny was to be fulfilled elsewhere. Still, I took out my map and made plans to visit the school. I had to discover for myself.

The Haight District was a bus ride further into the city. When

Psychedelic Wild Child

I found the school, which occupied an old apartment building, I explained my situation and asked if someone could show me around. The people there were happy to let me observe, but everyone was occupied. I looked around myself, although there was nothing there that really hooked me or took my interest. And the kids hovered in groups that didn't feel particularly welcoming. As I walked out the door, some burned-out junkies were hanging around on the streets panhandling for a fix, and I decided San Francisco had seen better days. The Haight was no longer flush with creative young minds, but full of deviated souls getting low on heroin and doing nothing I considered inspirational. Ducky had been right: I was not going to find anything new to raise my consciousness here. It was a big letdown, but I decided to take a little more time to see other parts of the city as long as I was here.

Ducky lived in a walkable neighborhood not too far from North Beach with lots of interesting little shops. One day I stopped at a middle-eastern bakery, where a man watched me eying the treats made of pistachio, dates, and delicate, crisp pastry in the glass case. Feeling his eyes on me, I looked over and found a very tan guy with long, straight, dark locks held back by a leather thong around his forehead donned in buckskins. He had a soulful sense about him. He seemed so confident, with a sense of calm and wholeness, that intrigued me. We began an easy conversation as I waited for my pastry and continued out together. As he lived nearby, he offered to take me on a tour of the neighborhood, and we talked about my journey. I felt at peace with him; he wasn't lusting after me, and he spouted little bits of spiritual truths to accentuate our conversations. He seemed to be just living in the moment, and his plans for the future were uncertain. We spent a few days together, but in the end, he was just a man attracted to my sensuality. While I enjoyed the attention, stimulating conversation, and sex, it was not enough to hold me. He gave no inclination to want to make it more than what it was, a passing interest. I knew my destiny was not here in San Francisco.

After three weeks there, I stuck my thumb out on the Pacific Coast Highway heading to Los Angeles, the city of the angels—the place where James said, "You will just have to come out and see for yourself." The last destination on my list of possibilities. A beige and white Volkswagen van whose license plate bore "MAGICBUS" stopped to give me a ride. This seemed like an omen. A slight, kindly, balding middle-aged man (of course, I thought he was an old man) rolled down the window and asked, "Where are you headed?"

I replied, "Are you going to LA?"

He said, "Yes, I am. Hop in. You need to be careful. I'll get you there safely." He was, in fact, a magician traveling from job to job up and down the coast. I gave him the address, 8301 Sunset Boulevard, and he said, "I know the area well."

After a couple of hours, the sun went down. He needed to rest, and I had yet to learn how to drive, so we pulled over into a rest area along the highway where we could sleep and have a bite.

Although it was compact, the van was roomy. Two benches folded down from the sides into single beds in the back. I watched as he pulled a gun out from under the seats and placed it under his pillow. He noticed me watching and said, "Don't be alarmed. This will keep us safe." I believed him. He was a gentleman who didn't come on to me and had even paid for dinner, so I lay down and fell asleep. We drove the entire next day, arriving in LA just after 9 p.m. Perhaps he was a guardian angel sent to keep me safe, showing me to the door where all the magic was really going to happen.

The Sunset Strip was animated, bustling, and filled with cars, bright lights, and colorful people enjoying the nightlife. In the midst of it all stood the Source Restaurant on the corner of Sunset and Sweetzer. Its patio was unlit and stacked with wrought iron tables and chairs dripping wet from a hosing, but I noticed lights on in the kitchen.

9

Dawnlight of the Age of Aquarian

At the back of the damp patio stood a small brick building. There was a round window at the top of the door. I walked up to it and knocked. The head of a man appeared with a white turban wrapped around it. With a look of disdain from flashing aqua eyes, he rudely snapped, "We're closed."

My heart sank. I could feel it in the pit of my stomach: what would happen if I was left there on the street?

"But wait a minute! I've come all the way from Chicago. My friends James and Roy invited me here," I pleaded hopefully. When James had left Chicago, all he could say was, "LA is where it's all happening. If you want to know what, come and find out." He had left me an address to write to him. But my crush on Roy had been the true deciding impetus that had pulled me to LA. Now I had arrived on August 1, 1972, the same date my dad had moved us into our new house and the same date that would mark many beginnings for me in the future. But on this day, I knew there was something more I had to find out. My heart had been magnetized by Roy's deep, spiritual soul and craved to expand into it.

The man at the window gave me a look of resigned disinterest and turned his back as another man stepped up and opened the door. He wore a turban, white shirt, and trousers topped by a dirty apron. They both seemed a little sweaty on this warm summer night, but it didn't seem to bother them.

He offered kindly, "My name is Horus. The restaurant is closed, and everyone is asleep at the Mother House. You can go crash in the teepee out back next to the Temple." Horus was soft-spoken with a friendly demeanor and an easy smile. "Don't be put off by Waterfall," he continued, referring to the man who couldn't be bothered and had reacted as if I were a bug. "We hold class in the morning. Someone will come to get you. I'll show you out to the teepee."

He led me through the dark dining room filled with wooden tables and chairs to the back door and then pointed to the left. "It's on the end of the Temple."

"What kind of class?" I responded.

"Oh, I thought you knew. We meet every morning before sunrise to catch the rising currents of universal life energy to meditate together. Father leads us in chanting and breathing exercises and comes down with the day's energies."

"Who is Father?" I wondered aloud, thinking there was so much more I needed to know.

Horus laughed. "There is a lot you're going to have to take on faith. You'll meet him in the morning. Meanwhile, you can rest back here."

Across from the back door stood a two-story redwood building he called the Temple, which sat atop the produce prep shed. I stepped onto the little cement patio to find a couple of tables and chairs, a strange-looking swing with no seat, and at the back against the dirt hillside, a cream-colored teepee. A large, stained-glass window in the shape of a six-pointed star shone down from the end of the Temple above the teepee. I pulled open the flap and stepped inside to find piles of pillows atop sheepskins and a stack of Mexican blankets. A cozy enchanting nest invited me to curl up in this little hidden nook off bustling Sunset Boulevard. Exhausted, I laid down and promptly fell fast asleep.

My eyes popped open from slumber in the middle of the night to see hovering several feet above me a face, described to me all my life as the face of God. His penetrating blue eyes gazed softly but directly into mine with curiosity. Long, silver and gold curled locks fell from around his face. In a lullaby to my soul, he whispered, "I was told someone was out here. Go back to sleep. I'm only checking in to be sure you are okay."

That was the first time I saw Father Yod. James and Roy had traveled to Los Angeles to seek out this man and what he had created. But neither had ever mentioned a hint of Father to me. They'd only spoken of a vegetarian restaurant they'd worked at.

△ ▽ △ ▽

I awoke to a still-dark morning, a bit overwhelmed. "Rise and shine," said a bright, happy face who suddenly popped through the flap and as quickly disappeared. The air was still a little cooler at that time of day, which felt good. It also had a crisp, piney smell I later learned was eucalyptus, a new experience for this Chicagoan. I popped my head out to witness a flurry of activity. Dozens of people all dressed in white were scurrying around the unpaved, gravelly parking lot next to the teepee, making preparations for class. Sheepskins were laid atop Mexican blankets on the dusty ground with pillows, set up in large concentric circles leaving a wide-open space in the center. I dressed hastily—I didn't want to miss this—and grabbed a sheepskin and blanket from the teepee, found an empty spot on the outer ring, and sat down to wait for class to begin. All the women were wearing white dresses, and I suddenly wished I had put on a skirt instead of my patched, blue-jean bell-bottoms.

Seated around me, everyone was focused with their eyes closed, practicing breathing exercises or meditating. I eagerly anticipated how this was done and what it all meant while looking around the circle, trying to visually locate James or Roy in the dim light. My concentration was broken when Father Yod emerged from the back of the restaurant in simple white pants, shirt, and shawl with bare feet. A white turban hugged his flowing gold and silver hair. A giant of a man, his long strides quickly brought him into the center of the circle. His presence was magnificent, emanating a bright aura surrounding his solid six-foot-four frame, a body that was of a man much younger than his fifty-one years. All I had blindly searched for in a teacher, in a school, in a spiritual foundation was standing right there in front of me, and I began to feel a growing sense of déjà vu and synchronicity.

Father Yod's teaching method was spontaneous; he would "come down" with the information he tapped into during deep meditation. Today it's called channeling. We chanted Yod He Vau He (pronounced yode-hay-vaw-hay) which is the Tetragrammaton, the Hebrew ineffable name of God, using melodies from songs like the Hebrew national anthem and old movie scores to chant them. Then all went quiet for a few minutes. Father Yod began, "The ascending currents of universal life energy begin after midnight. One must wake long before sunrise to catch them in their purest form before everyone else is awake spreading their negative thought patterns. Everything is energy, and all energy carries a vibration, positive or negative. Upon awakening, you must exercise your body and take a cold shower to rinse off the negative energy that attaches itself while sleeping." I got the feeling he was speaking directly to me. He continued to speak about Eastern and Western spiritual traditions; vegetarianism; health; relationships; wearing all white to reflect the light; and new ways to live, think, and deal with the Maya, the world of illusion around us. We were ultimately responsible for our own reality. We had to be consciously conscious of the effects of our causes in order to complete our wheel of karma. And we needed to learn to live in the world but not be of it.

By the time the sun was about to rise, we all stood and locked arms as he instructed—left hand up, right hand down, legs spread apart—to perform the Star Exercise followed by the Pineal Wave. This was a breathing exercise with 108 deep rapid breaths, called the breath of fire, followed by three deep, full inhales and exhales with heels together, sending all of the negativity in our beings down our spines and through our heels to the center of the earth to be cleansed. We then inhaled the clean pure breath of the day into our bodies to nourish our souls.

We continued to watch the sunrise over the Sunset Strip. We were in the world but not of it. I felt my awareness shifting, recognizing everything as cause and effect, being reborn into a new consciousness. My entire being was engulfed by all of these new thoughts and answers to long-lingering questions, and all these beautiful souls, living and working together in harmony, so scrupulously clean. It was heaven on earth; a dream become reality. Father eclipsed all my thoughts of James and Roy for the time being.

After class, everyone wandered off to their respective houses or prepared to work in the restaurant. Father climbed up to the attic of the Source and sent word for me to join him. I headed upstairs immediately with much excitement. The attic access was through the men's bathroom of the restaurant, where a ladder was bolted to the wall leading to a square hatch in the ceiling that hinged up. He lived upstairs of the restaurant with Ahom, his twenty-three-year-old wife. Everyone affectionately called her Mother.

"Welcome, daughter," greeted Ahom, who was waiting for me. She reached her arms around me for a big welcoming hug. She felt like a long-lost sister, bearing a similar resemblance to me, with long, dark, curly hair and brown eyes. My Jewdar sensed her Jewish heritage.

"The ceiling is very low up here, so be careful and don't hit your head," she warned. I followed her, stooped, and crawled from the office at the top of the stairs into the private chamber. Father sat in lotus with eyes closed in front of an altar with a triangular mirror at his back. Many curious objects decorated this space: little bronze statues of Indian deities, crystals, and a small pile of books on a thick, cream wool carpet. A golden bowl with a single gardenia floating in its waters sat on the altar scenting the tiny room. The walls were draped from the peaked ceiling with a beautiful, scrolling white and gold brocade fabric all the way down to the floor on the sides. Ahom motioned for me to sit down next to her on a sheepskin in front of him.

Parking lot meditation, I'm on the bottom right with my long hair and back to the camera..

10

Finding My Spiritual Father

Father's eyes opened to mine. My whole being lit up with joy from the powerful energy he sent emanating into me.

He smiled wide, "Welcome my daughter. How did you come so far to find me?"

I retold my journey and essentially how I was looking for some kind of spiritual school to attend. And after hearing his wisdom in class that morning, there was no question I had found it.

"What is your name, daughter?" he asked.

"Dawn," I replied softly.

"You already have a beautiful name. I don't think I can change that," he wondered aloud.

I remembered him speaking about starting a new life in the Brotherhood of the Source in class. Everyone who joined the Family would be given a new name. Our new last name was "the Aquarian."

"But I really want to be reborn with a new name," I pleaded.

He closed his eyes for a moment, then re-opened them. "All right. Then I shall call you Dawnlight, as I can only add to your beautiful name. Dawnlight the Aquarian." Father looked so happy and satisfied after naming someone, and I would witness this repeated over again many times.

Looking back, it would have been appropriate for me to finally be fully Dawn. All my life I had been Didi, hard as I tried to get people to call me otherwise. But that was to be for another time.

Father continued, "We are living the Ten Commandments for the Age of Aquarius, opening the gates to the New Age." Father brought down these Ten Commandments and wrote about them in a book he titled *Liberation*, which could be bought in the dining room of the restaurant for $1.00, just enough to cover the cost of publishing. He often said, "The word of God cannot be bought and sold. We are changing the parameters of life; we have made our own society and ideals, and are responsible only to ourselves and each other." It was our own culture—or some would say *cult*—but we were a good cult. The Piscean Age was dead to us, along with all of its antiquated dogmas and tenets.

Ten Commandments
For the Age of Aquarius

1. Obey and live by the teachings of your Earthly Spiritual Father
2. Love your Earthly Spiritual Father more than yourself.
3. Harm not one of your body parts either by neglect, food, drink, or knife.
4. Allow each vibration to complete its own cycle without interference.
5. Possess nothing that you don't need and share all that you have.
6. The man and his woman are one, let nothing separates them.
7. Squander not your creative force in lust but come together only when the three vibrations of the physical, the mental, and the emotional are in harmony with Spiritual Love.
8. Each morning join your vibration with the ascending currents of Universal Life Energy, using the keys that your Earthly Spiritual Father has taught you.
9. Do every act energetically, intelligently, truthfully, and lovingly.
10. When these commandments are mastered, leave the house of your Earthly Spiritual Father and do the work of your Heavenly Father.

We sat talking for a while longer getting to know each other, and soon Father wanted to go downstairs to the restaurant. He held court at a table in the corner by the window next to the front door. The morning rush had just passed as Ahom and I joined him for a breakfast of fresh fruit with yogurt, mixed nuts, and raw honey served in heavy wooden bowls. Everyone who worked at the restaurant was part of the Family, so anyone who was not busy with their work clustered around to listen to Father. During breakfast, Father spoke about the importance of diet and eating as much raw food as possible in order to receive the living enzymes and essential nutrients our bodies needed. He explained how vital it was to eat organic foods grown without any pesticides or chemical fertilizers, and how fifteen minutes after fresh fruit and vegetables were cut open, they began to lose their vitality. These were the early days of the organic world; "raw" and "organic" weren't even buzzwords yet.

Father said there would be a place in the Mother House for me, but it might take a few days to arrange. After breakfast, I was driven in one of the Family's red-and-white Volkswagen vans to a modern, white brick home in the nearby Los Feliz area called The Source Arts. A group of artistic Source members lived there. The house bore a Moroccan theme accented with mosaic tile and stained glass. The front steps led up through a multi-tiered sunny garden. I was told I could stay here temporarily until a spot in the Mother House was available. The Family was scattered in several houses at that time, still growing into itself. Everyone chipped in for the rent and shared expenses.

After a night on the couch at Source Arts, I was loaned a white dress and rode to class in a van filled with new brothers and sisters. Class was a repeat of the prior morning, but full of new wisdom, ringing bells of truth in my soul. After class was over, I was invited to the Mother House, where the enchantment transfixed me.

The Motherhouse, also in Los Feliz, was originally called the Chandler mansion, built by a newspaper magnate for his wife. It hosted twenty-four rooms, five bathrooms, an attic, a pool, plus a two-bedroom coach house above a six-car garage! The estate itself had been reduced from its original multiple acreages to about one. It was still magnificent though, an old, russet-brick house surrounded by a wide lawn and a lovely landscaped garden reminiscent of old Hollywood.

A long, tree-lined brick driveway wound from the curb into the property to a parking area in front of the garage. I stepped out of the van and saw a group of children funneling into the stairwell of the garage. A sister pointed out that up those stairs led to where all the children lived together. The garage doors were open. Inside I saw a workshop with a giant loom consuming an entire parking spot. A man with bushy, blond hair bound by a headband sat at the loom weaving.

He looked up and smiled. "Do you weave?" he asked, seeing my fascination. "My name is Chekatec."

"I'm Dawnlight. I've always made things with my hands: sewing, beading, clay, and crafting. I've never tried weaving but would like to."

"I'd be happy to teach you how."

"Thanks, I'll look forward to that!" I eagerly responded.

The coach house sat next to an Olympic-size swimming pool, which was slightly elevated on a brick wall topped by a wrought iron fence.

Inside the fence was a bricked patio dotted with bushes and palms and a dozen or so naked people hanging out, swimming, lounging, and giving or receiving massages. Being introduced to my new Family members felt like meeting long-lost friends, except they had new names: Heaven, Venus, Palm, Ra, Omne, Isis, Osiris, Soma, Madonna, Lotus, and Paralda. We made an instant connection, and I felt a sense of deep déjà vu and belonging.

And then I spotted Roy just outside the pool walking up the driveway. Ahom informed me that he was now called Pythias. My heart leaped. In class, I had noticed him with another woman—a bit of a letdown. They were sitting in the inner circle at Father's feet. What mattered more to me now was that I had found Father Yod, my spiritual Father. His wisdom was all I had been seeking and there were so many other beautiful souls here to discover. But Pythias had taken my heart.

Pythias saw me, broke out in a smile, rushed over, and wrapped his long arms around me with a warm, welcoming hug. "I'm so glad you're here," he whispered in my ear. He smelled of food, having just finished his morning shift at the restaurant as head chef. A thrill of excitement burst through me. As it set in, I struggled to keep my emotions in check, not wanting to seem overly eager. Mutte [pronounced muh-tay] ran up behind him, eagerly seeking an introduction. She was tiny next to him but pulled back her shoulders which emphasized her enormous, mismatched breasts, and shook her wispy, blond hair. With a big, bright smile, her elven eyes keenly aware of the loving attention he was giving me, she immediately interlinked her arms in his, holding tight while giving me a fixed gaze relaying the silent message: Pythias was hers. Still in my cloud of enchantment, I gracefully hugged her in welcome, not allowing myself or anyone else to recognize my deep disappointment.

"Why don't I show you around?" Mutte offered. Pythias smiled and excused himself saying, "That's a great idea. I'm going to go clean up."

We strolled up the brick path through the sprawling lawn to tour this amazing mansion. The house towered three stories up to a steeply peaked roof with cottage window accents and trailing ivy. Mutte did most of the talking; she was quite a chatterbox, describing the twenty-four rooms and who lived where.

We entered the house through several sets of French doors into a large, open, polished wood entryway. The walls were lined in rich mahogany panels bordered with inset molding. To the right was the meditation room. I peeked into the big, open space with high ceilings, painted white with bits of gold trim. The scent of sandalwood incense lingered in the air. Floor-to-ceiling windows were draped with sheers, but no furniture was in this room. Several people were scattered on pillows around the thick, cream-colored wool carpet, reading and meditating. They looked up, curious about the new face.

Horus from the restaurant was there. He asked, "How are you liking everything so far?"

I stepped in and smiled shyly at them all and said, "I've only ever seen a house like this in the movies, and I'm blown away to find myself standing here. Father is the most interesting and dynamic person I've ever met!" They all laughed knowingly. Mutte led me past the large marble fireplace opposite the windows. Back out in the hall, a grand wooden staircase with carved balusters rose beside the front doors. We ascended to a wide balcony stretching above the front doors with a bench and more windows overlooking the front lawn. Several more steps on the opposite side led to the second floor.

11

Dawnlight Sheds on Bonadea

Pythias and Mutte's room sat at the top of the stairs. It was immense, with wainscoting and wallpaper lining two walls and windows covering the other two, broken up by a big wood-framed fireplace. Mutte beamed quite smugly as we entered. I glanced at their big bed and suddenly envied Mutte. She was there with him, and I wasn't. I kept shoving this feeling away, knowing that I needed to accept what was. They shared a bathroom with the room next door in which Damian, manager of the Source restaurant, lived with the golden-haired beauty Aquariana. He and Pythias had been lifelong pals, both from Mississippi whose families had moved to Chicago. Mutte and Aquariana had also been childhood friends in LA.

The bathroom walls and floor were covered in simple, octagonal white tile with polished dark wood trim. The tubs in all the bathrooms were so long you could stretch out completely. I imagined myself floating there! Several other large suites were also on this floor, with several people living in each one.

Mutte said, "The attic's being transformed into more living spaces. There are somewhere around fifty people living here. Now I'll show you the kitchen. It's down through the old servant's staircase."

We tread down the dark, narrow passage to step out into a huge, bright, airy room. This kitchen looked like something out of an *Upstairs/Downstairs* movie set. An entire wall was lined with big metal doors bearing heavy lever handles. Behind each door was a different compartment of one massive refrigerator! Mutte pulled one of the levers to reveal cases of fresh green lettuce, fruits, cheese, and dates, a vegetarian's fantasy. It smelled so inviting, and there was such an abundance of food! She reached in and pulled out a date. I looked at it strangely because I'd never seen one before.

She looked at me in surprise and asked, "Don't you know what this is?"

"No," I replied, staring at the small, brown, oblong fruit, wondering if it was anything like a giant raisin.

"You're in for a treat! They're sweet, creamy, and delicious. Be careful of the big pit inside." She handed me the sticky, brown date, and as I bit into it, it melted in my mouth with buttery ambrosian delight. It became my new treat obsession; often when I was in the kitchen, I would snag one of these pieces of heaven to savor.

A woman was standing in the center of the kitchen at an island twenty feet long, chopping vegetables on the thick, butcher-block top. Open storage shelves beneath were stacked with wooden bowls. A man was washing dishes at the restaurant-sized triple sink under the windows of one wall. Yards of white cabinets above, below, and around the room left me wondering what was in them. An adjacent butler's pantry was lined with glass cabinets, displaying a myriad of handmade ceramic mugs. A large coffee urn sat on the tiled counter by the sink. None of the hippie houses I'd ever visited had this much organization and style!

A swinging pantry door with a porthole window showed us into the dining room. There, a shiny, black grand piano stood in an alcove lined with more sheer, draped, floor-to-ceiling windows. Opposite stood a fireplace big enough for the children to hold a tea party in, framed with fancy, carved-wood scrollwork and a marble mantelpiece.

Pythias, looking fresh in clean whites, with long damp hair laying over his shoulders, met up with us and asked, "Are you hungry? Maybe you'd like to have lunch with us?"

"After that kitchen tour, how can I resist?" I gushed.

Mutte smiled and turned to the kitchen, leaving Pythias and me to talk. Others surrounded us though, curiously asking questions about who I was and where I was from, and not allowing us a chance to speak alone. Mutte soon returned with beautiful salads in large wooden bowls. "These are Yod He Vau He salads. A rainbow of avocado, tomatoes, alfalfa sprouts, red onions, purple cabbage, eggplant, and the restaurant's signature Source lemon herb salad dressing." We sat down at the large antique dining room table for the feast.

Pythias said, "I hope you're going to stay. You seem to like our house and Father. I'd be happy if you did."

I answered, "Yes! I can see why you and James had to be here. I had no idea that Father Yod and the Family were what I'd been searching for. I thought I was looking for a new kind of school, but I'm ready for this new life and excited to leave the past behind. I do look forward to living in the Mother House. I can't believe you never told me about all of this. It's incredible!"

Pythias beamed from the other side of the table, nodding, and said, "Yes, you've found your new school—just a different kind." Mutte was paying very close attention to our every little gesture, response, and expression. With all of the other thoughts running through my head, the jealousy and disappointment didn't matter.

"Where is James?" I changed the subject.

"He lives down the hall with my sister, Mushroom," Mutte was sure to let all intentions be clear.

"He is now called Ramacharaka and works the juice bar at the restaurant during the day. You'll see him soon," Pythias added.

△ ▽ △ ▽

I was recruited to work at the restaurant immediately. My job was to assist in the dining room bussing, cleaning, and setting up tables. Most of the waitresses were women, and most of the kitchen crew were men. There was a flow in how everything worked and how everyone worked together. I loved feeling a part of this. After the festival in Colorado, I daydreamed about living in a spiritual commune with a healthy lifestyle of pureness and truth, and here I was. None of the communes I had experienced in Chicago could begin to compare. I did have some interactions with Ramacharaka, but they were brief, and he was preoccupied with his work and, whenever Mushroom was around, with her.

Father was not your everyday guru demanding total draconian devotion. Everything was structured like a real family. Yes, he commanded respect, and we followed his instruction or could leave. Everything he taught resonated with absolute truth for me. He welcomed our questions and made himself available, ready to speak about anything. Once he even made a big point about the right way to hang toilet paper in the bathroom, with the end sheet hanging in front! We had a big laugh over that. Nothing he spoke of was too mundane or untouchable, and he made everything fun.

Three days in, I realized I hadn't yearned for or even thought about having a cigarette! I was so mesmerized and taken in by this new way of life and Father Yod's teachings that I was sucking up all of his wisdom instead of smoke.

At the same time, I was invited to move into a room in the Mother House shared by Boaz, who crafted knee-high leather moccasins; Madonna; and their baby, Maize. He welcomed me with an intense gaze from large, dark, thoughtful eyes, focusing from under a thick bush of dark hair blending into his beard. Madonna, a singer and sweet mother was tall and sylph-like, with long, flowing, sandy hair. She warmly welcomed me with a hug. Their room was down at the end of the hall from Pythias and Mutte.

Several days later, Arelich [pronounced are-el-ick] moved in with us. He was formerly Sky Saxon from the rock band The Seeds, famous for their song "You're Pushin' Too Hard." Arelich and Boaz had been friends before the Family. He was very sweet and quite the ladies' man, with a boyish charm yet an old man's face with sad, worried eyes. He was burned out; his thoughts were flighty, and he often stared blankly into space. This was the first of Arelich's forays into the Family; he would float in and out many times over the years.

His presence was a bit weird for me. With his bedroll only inches from mine on the floor, he soon set his attention on me. I was flattered and accepted his advances—old habits, I guess. He was my first groupie experience before I knew what that was, but the sex just didn't feel right. I no longer wanted to have sex for its own sake—plus I was still pining for Pythias.

After being there a week, I visited Father Yod after class above the restaurant and said, "I don't feel right. I need an entirely new name because Dawnlight still doesn't feel like a break from my past." I wanted to forget the girl who fell for the guy in Chicago, but I couldn't say that to him, even though I think he sensed it. I added, "I also don't feel like I fit in with Boaz, Madonna, and especially Arelich."

Father said, "Dawnlight is a beautiful name and suits you. I'm sorry you don't feel it."

He closed his eyes to meditate. After a few moments, he laughed and said, "You will now be known as Bonadea. Venus has moved up to the attic and has some extra space; I'll arrange for her to share it with you."

The name Bonadea came from an Atlantean priestess who lived in an ivory tower, and now, here I was moving into the new tower space with Venus. It felt like my new life had begun in earnest. I was so excited, my skin felt like it was vibrating. One of the Family's VW vans took me back to the Mother House. I returned to Boaz and Madonna's room to gather my belongings and inform them of my good news. They seemed happy enough that there would be one less person in their space and wished me well. I left them to deal with Arelich's sad puppy-dog face.

12

Living in LA, The Source Way

My green aluminum-framed backpack and a cardboard breadbox from the restaurant were stuffed to the gills with the remainder of my meager possessions. I had few to start with since traveling. Newly added to them were a couple of old Victorian nightgowns, a vintage, satin, long-sleeved chemise, a petticoat, and a few tops—all in white—from a swap-meet shopping trip with Ahom—plus the book *Liberation*, written by Father Yod.

I climbed the dark back hallway to the attic. The bare wood stairs creaked on every other step. The light at the top was dim, the unpainted, dark redwood deadening the light coming in from the gabled windows. Under the peak of the roof, bare crossbeams ran the length of it. It smelled like pristine, warmed wood with no humans around to eclipse the aroma, making me feel like one of the first souls to settle here. The attic stretched the entire length of the house. Far down by the end, I could see white sheets hanging from the rafters in an enclosure. *That must be it.* I stepped up my pace, and soon a face framed with thick, straight, dark hair appeared from behind the curtain with a big smile.

"Dawnlight! I heard you coming! Come on down!" Venus shouted.

"Thanks, but I'm Bonadea now," I gleefully answered.

"Cool, that was fast! Glad you didn't get lost. The house can be a maze," she replied.

"I've been fascinated by the Mother House since my first visit and am still getting used to the idea that I live here. It's like living a fairy-tale," I said.

Venus sat on her bed, waving me in and motioning to the other side of the little enclosure, where a thick, padded-cotton bed mat lay.

"There are some hooks on the wall to hang things on, and the curtain at the bottom of the wall covers a storage space to stash anything else behind," Venus relayed.

A small altar with a triangular mirror and two candlesticks in front of it separated the two mats. I'd noticed that every room had an altar with a pyramid mirror, as they were called.

"What are these triangular mirrors all about?"

"It's a tool used in one of the meditation exercises we practice called the Mystic Road, a focusing exercise that continues daily for sixteen weeks with a new task each week. It starts at five minutes a day and leads up to an hour a day," she replied.

"Am I going to have to do that?" I asked.

"Father will let you know when you're ready."

I busied myself unpacking an army-surplus down sleeping bag, a couple of pairs of jeans, a few of my homemade India-print blouses and skirt, some shampoo, conditioner, and Dr. Bronner Peppermint soap. In addition, I had my sandals, wallet, notebook, and pen. I figured out what to put where while Venus watched. Folding up the jeans and clothes that I wouldn't be wearing, I put them in my backpack and placed my new white pieces on the hooks provided. Everything else went in the cardboard box that slid behind the curtain with the backpack.

"You don't have many clothes," Venus noted. "I noticed some of your old ones look handmade. Your handiwork?"

"Yes. I used to love to take India-print bedspreads and transform them."

"I know a great fabric shop where we can get homespun fabric, and I have a sewing machine. There's a fun flea market on Santa Monica on the weekend. Have you started working in the restaurant yet?"

"Yes, I'm now in the kitchen making juices on the morning shift," I responded, laughing.

"Good. You'll have some money to go shopping," Venus cheered.

I looked around the small space and noticed some pillows with ornate beadwork and embroidery that were trimmed with lace sitting on her bed.

"Did you make those?" I inquired. Venus beamed back and nodded yes. I could see we were going to get on just fine!

Venus had a gypsy nature: independent, streetwise, free-spirited, and clever. She was also a verified genius. I loved watching her as she was thinking. She was like a clock ticking. Each move of the hand could be seen on her face, and her eyes moved back and forth as she came to some mental conclusion. She had been a hairdresser in Hollywood and had made many friends in the "business," having joined the Family only a few months before. At almost my height, we both shared the dark hair/dark eye thing: mine curly, hers straight as a pin. We were both curvy girls too, with a little soft padding—although by no means fat. But Father Yod wanted us both to slim down and often put us on different diets to do so, including the cottage cheese-and-melon diet, the steamed-vegetables-only diet, and various juice fasts. I even ended up on several thirty-day water fasts!

Looking back, the truth is that all this set me up for a lifetime of not feeling good enough about my curves, and to this day, it has made it much harder for me to deal with my self-image. It has always left me feeling as if I'm never thin enough, fit enough, or a perfect woman just as I am. But a little bit of Jim Baker remained in Father Yod, a man born of a certain era who had particular ideas of how a woman should look. He had been a World War II decorated hero, jujitsu champion, and restauranteur previously on the Sunset Strip with the Old World and Aware Inn restaurants. But Jim had also been a man who had left his wife and three sons and had been known as a womanizer. I forgive him for his antiquated judgements, but I will never forget.

I did love to prepare food with Venus. Once, we were making salad, and I curiously watched as Venus poured out olive oil, sesame oil, apple cider vinegar, and tamari sauce without measuring them into a jar. She said, "I make my own salad dressing." It was such an *a-ha* moment for me: salad dressing had always come from a bottle; it was not something one could make. She then sprinkled our salads liberally with sesame seeds and nutritional yeast, and it was the most delicious salad I'd ever tasted. She also used the same dressing over steamed veggies— even better!

As I made my new clothes, others took interest in my styles and skills. Soon, my talents were tapped to make clothing for others in the Family, and I went on to become one of our more prolific clothing designers. I got to know all the Family's haunts for fabrics, like International Silks and Woolens and The Homespun House, and I would find antique trims and other bits from local flea markets like the one on Santa Monica that Venus and Ahom had introduced me to.

△ ▽ △ ▽

One of the more fascinating aspects of living in the City of Angels was the number of spiritual centers amassed there. These resources were not as readily available to me in Chicago. Before becoming Father Yod, Jim Baker had taken advantage of this, seeking a deeper meaning of life in LA. In Topanga Canyon, he had discovered Paul Bragg, Gypsy Boots, and Jack Lalanne, who were known as "the Nature Boys." They all shared the same ideas about health and raw food with great enthusiasm. These ideas were the basis of Father Yod's first restaurant, the Aware Inn, on Sunset Boulevard.

Then one day, Jim was invited to a party where he had a chance meeting with the newly immigrated Yogi Bajan. The Indian government had sent the Yogi to LA to further the Sikh religion. The two men caught each other's attention—they could see each other eye to eye, as the Yogi was as physically imposing a man as Jim. Then when Jim was about to leave, the Yogi stopped him by grabbing his arm and insisting he join him for meditation the next morning. This would lead to a life-changing regime for Jim—his first step into true devotion to spiritual studies with the Yogi, whom he now considered to be his spiritual father.

At about the same time, Jim had come across the book *The Secret Teachings of All Ages* by Manley P. Hall of the Philosophical Research Society, whose headquarters were in LA. Jim sought out the author after reading it, as he liked to get to the core of things. They developed a good friendship, to the point that Mr. Hall bestowed a list of names of souls who would find their way to Jim's "family." When Father Yod gave us names, he used this list, as well as some of the Aquarian names that had come down to him.

At the time he and Robin, now Ahom, were to be married, he sought out Ann Davies, then head of the Builders of the Adytum, or

Psychedelic Wild Child

B.O.T.A, a school and order based on the Western Mystery tradition of Tarot. She agreed to officiate if they took classes, so Jim learned about Paul Foster Case, the B.O.T.A. founder, as well as the basics and history of Tarot cards. Later on, the teachings of Foster Case would become incorporated into our Source Family curriculum, particularly *The Book of Tokens*, meditations on the major arcana of the Tarot. Father Yod eventually added a page to the book on the Death card, a piece we all transcribed into our own volumes:

The true nature of this death power is indicated by the number thirteen. This is a number in Hebrew of two words. One means unity; the other means love. The one power from which all things proceed, the love power, is the cause of all attractions and affinities. It is also the death power, which brings about the dissolution of the physical bodies. These are not two antagonistic powers, one making for life, the other for death. There are only opposite-having manifestation forms of "Yahowha."

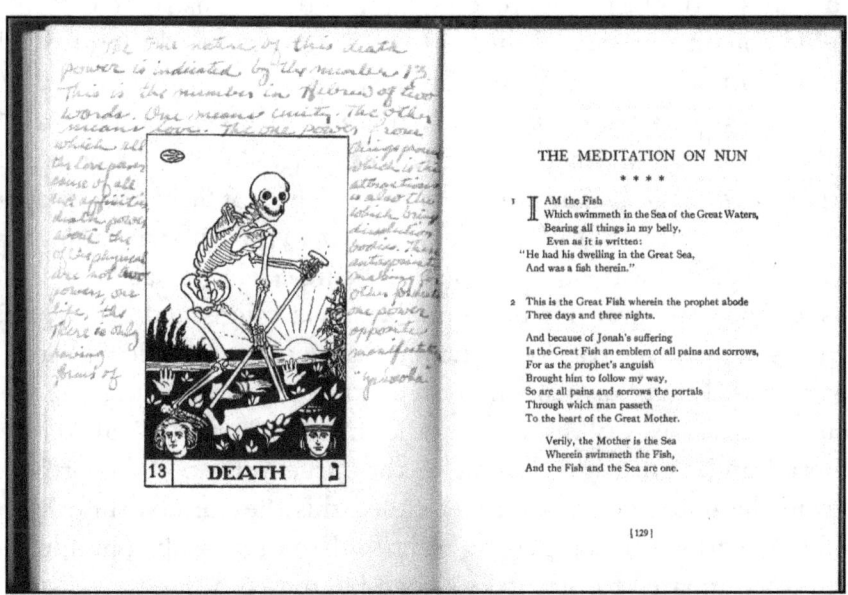

Father Yod had divined a method of practicing the Tarot in our daily lives by using the major arcana cards, starting at the first, the Magician, on the first day of the month. Each day corresponded with a card until reaching the Fool card, whose number is zero. We learned about the symbolism of the cards and what their esoteric meanings were, instead of using them as a fortune-telling device. "It is a book of life," Father Yod would say, "All of the teachings of life can be found in the Tarot."

One day, Father sent Venus and me to the Theosophical Society Library headquarters in Pasadena. He knew others before him in the occult world had "come down" with similar information as he had and was curious to see if what he was tapping into was substantiated by them.

Entering the front door, I looked up into an enormous, old English-style library. Its oversized, ornate wooden front desk hosted several sets of peering eyes to greet and watch over anyone entering the front door. Bookshelves lined the walls two stories high, iron spiral staircases led to the second level, and sturdy wooden ladders were scattered along the stacks for easy access. Card catalogs sat across from the reception desk in their myriad drawers, and several small, glass-doored, antique wood cases containing ancient tomes were scattered around the perimeter of the room. In the center were rows of long, worn wooden tables and chairs with green glass reading lamps liberally distributed.

We sought out several authors we were particularly fond of, the foremost of whom was Mabel Collins, author of *Light on the Path* and *Through the Gates of Gold*. Anxiously, we skipped over to the card catalog to find other volumes by her. Ms. Collins was one of the lesser-known mystics and founders of the Theosophical Society when they were formed in 1875. Helena Blavatsky, a Russian immigrant, had elbowed her way in and ended up being celebrated as their senior mystic. She was given far more applause via salons and other public displays because she was so exotic, but Ms. Collins was the real deal. It was rumored that Blavatsky had even stolen all she was teaching from someone else. Ms. Collins, on the other hand, "channeled" all her own material and always gave credit to the "true author," who provided it from the unseen realms. Father called this the voice within. Mabel Collins's works were simple and right to the point—only a hundred or so pages compared to Blavatsky's head-tripping thousands.

Ms. Collins' other books were not on the regular shelf where her popular volumes were, so I approached the imposing front desk to inquire. To my surprise, the cheerful, gray-bunned lady answered my question, saying, "Those books are far too precious. We have only a few volumes and don't lend them out. But you are welcome to read them here. They are in that small case just across from the card catalogs."

I practically ran to it, reverently opening the glass door to peer inside. When I peeked back at her, she smiled with a knowing, matronly amusement. I found a few volumes, plopped down on the floor right beside the case, began to pore over them, and sat there all day. Venus kept herself occupied in other stacks doing the same. When it was closing time, the gray-bunned lady came over and said, "It's time to go home."

I was so disappointed. "I was really getting into *The Idyll of the White Lotus*!"

The library matron could see this and offered, "I will allow you to take this one volume with you, but you must promise to return it in one week's time. Then I will know if I can trust you."

"Oh, yes! You can count on me. I'll treat it as a precious treasure!"

Venus and I returned the next week with the book, proving our trust. She then allowed us to borrow others too. I wondered if she could tell how grateful I was for her kindness.

The Bodhi Tree on Melrose Avenue in West Hollywood was a bookstore we used to frequent for incense and also to browse the shelves. It was a full-service metaphysical bookstore. If there was something new and cutting edge, it was there. If it was something older and valued, it was there—except, of course, the rare volumes that could only be found in private libraries. Even then, they had a used bookstore next door where we occasionally unearthed treasures.

Eugene Ferson's book *Science of Being* was one we came across. It cost $60 back then, very expensive for a book. The cover was bound in brown, crocodile-etched leather, and the pages were a very delicate parchment with gilt edges. A red ribbon ran through the binding as a bookmark, and it was sold in a gold cardboard box with a protective clear plastic cover. Not everyone in the Family could afford this volume, but there were several floating around, so some found a way to get it. In fact, Father Yod was so inspired that he combined kundalini yoga breathing techniques with the Star Exercise that Mr. Ferson prescribed.

Another author Venus and I cherished was Corinne Heline, who wrote *The Sacred Science of Numbers*. When we discovered she was still alive and in a nursing home in Santa Monica, the two of us endeavored to find her and have a visit. We were told at the reception desk she was confined to her bed, blind, and didn't hear very well, but when we walked into the room, she was alone—and having a lively conversation with invisible beings!

She turned to us and instantly remarked loudly in my direction, "Oh, what a beautiful halo you have glowing around your head!" She was referring to a necklace of Aurora Borealis crystal beads I wore around my forehead. She began to tell us about the invisible friends she was speaking to, and we regaled her with stories of Father and the Family for as long as they would let us stay, which was only about an hour. We returned several times, cherishing those moments more each time. On our last visit, we decided she needed to be in a more appreciative environment—one where she could spend the rest of her days with a family of enlightened souls in the physical. In short, with us. We shared our wishes with her and told her that when the time came, she could experience an honored death with the Family, among those who would appreciate her and allow her three days to pass over. She liked the idea and was willing to go with us, and we got her in a wheelchair and made it as far as the parking lot before security guards caught up with us. Sadly, we were never allowed to visit her again. Born August 18, 1882, Corinne died July 26, 1975.

All of these experiences inspired me later to open a metaphysical bookstore of my own in Hawaii.

△ ▽ △ ∀

Class soon began being held at the Mother House—much cleaner and more private than the restaurant's parking lot. We all awoke every morning between 3 and 3:30 a.m. to prepare for class, doing exercises and taking cold showers to cleanse the residual negativity which clung to us in our dream state. This was followed by the perfect cup of coffee, with raw honey and half and half. Standing outside on the lawn in homespun dresses, robes, and shawls that insulated us in the cool morning darkness, we set the vibration for class, and in silence, we waited for Father's yellow-and-white VW van to arrive so we could greet him and Ahom.

Father's overall plan had been for everyone to move into the Mother House, and now we all had, except for him and his wife. We had all learned how little space was really needed for a bed mat and clothes.

The attic had become full of additional sheet-divided enclosures, with people doubled up in rooms. I think he saw the reality of the situation and decided he needed the privacy he had above the restaurant because whenever he was with the Family, he never had a moment to himself. Whoever was nearby would cluster around him to listen. But we were happy living all together at the Mother House, and of course, saw Father daily in class.

He also encouraged us to release our attachments to material possessions, which helped us live in such tight quarters. The Fifth Commandment for the Age of Aquarius is "Possess nothing that you do not need and share all that you have." We now pooled all our wages, so if one of us needed anything, all we had to do was place a request. This had become necessary because some still had not grasped the difference between wants and needs. As the restaurant was making a good profit, we all shared in it, as it paid for the rent and utilities of the Mother House as well as filled the enormous refrigerator with cases of organic produce in its kitchen. Father took requests for practical, everyday living expenses: toothbrushes, shoes, and altar supplies, but nothing extravagant. There was a daily group with requests lined up for him upstairs of the restaurant, where we could fit around fifteen people sitting cross-legged under the low-pitched ceiling on soft sheepskin rugs. When I could, I lined up with them. Not because I needed anything—I just wanted to be able to sit and listen to him. He never missed an opportunity to teach. When my turn came, he would laugh when I said I didn't need anything. I just wanted to be there to listen.

As I wasn't the only one with that motivation, Father Yod soon assigned Damian to handle these requests. Our leader needed some space from us all. Decisions about buying bigger things, like new cars, were made by Damian and Father together. In fact, we leased a fleet of red-and-white Volkswagen vans, and everyone else's vehicles were sold.

13

All Fall Down

One morning in class, Father Yod announced, "Celestial (the first Bonadea) has joined Ahom and me above the Source. A man can have more than one woman. It is relative in nature, such as with lions and apes. Woman serves her man and their family. Man serves God and provides for his women and family."

Even though the Sixth Commandment states, "The man and his woman are one; let nothing separate them," he explained that this could apply at the moment with each woman. So there could be more than one woman, a practice referred to many times in the Bible. Every day was a new adventure with him, a new play. We were experimenting with life. What didn't work the day before was abandoned for a new, better idea the next.

For anyone snickering and asking, "Oh, yes? Well, what about the women? Did they get to have more than one husband?", hold your horses and wait for a few.

Pythias liked this new plan. He found me after class and said, "Bonadea, you know I wanted to be with you from the moment you arrived. Now we can all be together. Let's go back to the Mother House. I can help you move your things."

I looked up at him with a wide smile and nodded yes, throwing my arms around him and showing more affection to him than I had dared to till that moment. Finally, a chance to be with him in the suite at the top of the grand staircase! I was over the moon.

Mutte, I could tell, was not. But I didn't care; I was more than eager to try this new concept. She made a stifled effort to accept me and crack open her heart a sliver. "Oh, we are going to be so close! When is your birthday?"

When I told her, she said, "We're almost twins! Mine is two days after yours!"

But we were worlds apart. I hung on to every word Father came down with, open to new ideas and change, but she did not seem to incorporate what he was teaching. We hobbled along for a few weeks, but Mutte became a real test. She would race to do everything for Pythias, like combing his hair, getting him his clothes, and making his food, which gave me little opportunity to do anything for him. He and I had to steal moments when she was busy to be together. I asked him, "Can't you talk to her and ask her to give me some space with you?"

"I have," he said, "but she's basically jealous and can't open her mind up to the idea of sharing."

Mutte could not break out of the traditional Piscean man/woman relationship and join our new Aquarian program. I tried to be open to all these new possibilities, but it didn't come easy for most of us to adapt to this idea.

It all came to a crashing halt when Mutte's mother called the cops. She wanted Mutte and her younger sister Mushroom back home and away from the Source. They were from LA and had been hanging around the Source for a couple of years, waitressing and listening to Father. They used to go home more, but when we moved into the Mother House, that stopped.

The sheriff came calling at the restaurant, and I was working as a waitress—the only underaged person to be found. Even though I had notarized permission from my parents to allow me to be there, I was taken into custody. Father Yod was furious about this. He said, "If you take her, you'll have to take me too," and they did. This must have been quite a scene for the customers!

The sheriffs seemed giddy at their catch. "This is only the beginning. Father Yod's going to be brought down, and you'll be sent back to Chicago to be with your parents, where you belong," one sheriff happily decreed.

I sat there stewing in the back seat of the patrol car and thinking they were wrong: that was *not* going to happen. It was all a big mistake. But I was processed in the sheriff's office and then driven in a van with steel-mesh-covered windows to *juvie*, a.k.a. juvenile hall.

We pulled up to a very dingy compound surrounded by a twelve-foot chain-link fence painted in depressing shades of gray-green with barred windows and doors. The sky in the yard could not help but reflect this gloominess, and my heart began to sink. Inside, there were no cells but rather rooms that consisted of four metal cots in each, and stainless-steel furnishings were scattered throughout. It was a jail. The heavy, hollow metal door to my room had a small window through which I could see the guards' faces as I was locked in. Sensing a bit of claustrophobia flickering in my brain, I fought my instincts to be calm. To make things even worse, there was a sour antiseptic smell permeating everything. It should have made me feel that the place was clean, but I couldn't help wondering if it was covering up something worse.

I was dressed in my all-white gown and a turban, which felt like a layer of protection from this alien environment. I couldn't blend in with the crowd. There were many other kids, all wearing a combination of T-shirts and bell-bottom jeans, who were very curious about me and asking lots of questions. As Father had taught us that all experience is either to teach or learn from, I thought it would be a good idea to see this as a teaching experience. I couldn't imagine what I'd learn . . . Patience? Humility?

I sat on my cot, closed my eyes, and began to chant softly. I was not going to be completely taken from my new life, so I willed myself to perpetuate it. I would be in the world but not of it.

"What are you singing?" a pretty, blond teenage girl on the cot next to me asked.

"The most ancient name of God, Yod He Vau He, or Yahowha, as it's pronounced. It's Hebrew," I answered.

"What does that mean?" She looked puzzled.

I rambled on in detail about what each letter, *yod, he, vau, he,* stood for and what the term's kabbalistic history was. I could tell she was bored and shut up. No one there really wanted to know the whole story. They were always curious about the new person—maybe another soul to commiserate with in that lonely place. It was mostly filled with runaway kids and those caught smoking pot or cutting school. But they left me alone for the most part after my conversation with the girl. I was the weirdo and far too serious.

The next morning at breakfast, there was a table with a tray of small cartons of milk and little paper boxes of cereal that were split open so the box could be used as a bowl. This was not what I would even call food. A stack of apples and bananas sat in the center of the table, so I opted for those and passed on the cereal. We were all ordered to go to "school" within the compound afterward. Of course, I had not attended for a long while, so it was a real effort for me to comply. I sat in the chair with a writing platform holding my head in my hand, completely uninterested.

Fortunately, they pulled me out early. The air travel back to Chicago was quickly arranged, and I was soon on my way to the airport in that van with metal mesh windows. I had spent a confusing and harrowing two days at the juvenile detention center before being shipped to Chicago on that late November day.

I arrived with only the clothes on my back, which I'd been wearing for the last two days, frustrated and cold because it was nearing winter. Although Mother had brought me a coat and was happy to have me home, she could see how unhappy I was.

"I don't want to wear my old clothes. I only wear white now," I stated, wanting to maintain my new persona. "And, everyone needs to call me Bonadea."

Mother said, "We can go shopping for fabric so you can make some new clothes, and we can also stop at the health food store." My parents were in as much of a quandary over the whole thing as I was. They tried, at least, to make me comfortable.

I called the Source every day to talk to Pythias. He could tell how helpless I felt and didn't know what to do.

"What happened in LA after I left?" I asked him.

Pythias was a man of few words. "Everything's cool."

"Well, what about Father? How did he get out of jail?" I pressed.

"They let him out. They couldn't hold him on any charges."

"What about Mutte and Mushroom?" I tried hard not to show frustration at his lack of detail.

"Oh, they went back to their mom for a night or two. But they came back," said the man of few words! "How are you holding up?"

"It's challenging. It's getting colder here, and I'm not seeing how I'm going to get out of this. My parents are asking me when I'm going to go back to school. I don't want to be anywhere but with you and Father," I complained.

He told Father how I felt, and Father sent him to Chicago a few days later with the directive, "Don't return until you're married."

Mother and I drove to the airport to collect Pythias. She knew he could cheer me up. I had been inconsolable.

△ ▽ △ ▿

Months earlier, my mother had flown to LA after I had called to say that I had found what I was looking for at the Source. I had described the restaurant, where I lived, Father, and the happiness it brought me. Of course, she had to come out to see for herself how all this had captured me, as it was not long after the Manson family murders, and "cults" were getting a bad name. My sister, Amy, tagged along, just as curious. Amy was scared of Father and didn't like him at all, believing that he'd taken her sister away from her, but Mother held a private meeting with Father Yod and found him to be "charming and grounded." She could see I was drug-free, not smoking, and working in the restaurant. I was learning about spirituality and responsibility and was living a healthy lifestyle—more points for California than Chicago. I was safe, cared for, and living in a beautiful place, and although she didn't agree with everything Father Yod was teaching, my life was saner than the one I had been living in Chicago. Father Yod and the Source Family had impressed her enough to let me stay.

△ ▽ △ ▿

Before Pythias arrived in Chicago, my dad took me to a psychiatrist on a quest to see if I had been brainwashed or had gone crazy. The shrink asked me questions about my life in LA and how the structure was set up, and then asked me to draw some pictures of my life there. She was impressed and told my parents that, in fact, I had a very healthy outlook on life, was not crazy, and most importantly, had not been brainwashed!

Pythias strutted out the airport doors in a blaze of whiteness, infusing me with hope and delight. I took in a deep breath of fresh air, supremely excited that I finally had some time alone with him without Mutte! Together, we would get me back to LA, Father, and my new life.

While Pythias stayed at my family's home, he and I continued to wake up at four in the morning to chant and meditate. We also showed my parents that we were in love, dedicated, and had to get married in order to return to The Source. And Pythias was determined to get me pregnant.

My parents were impressed by Pythias' charm, sincerity, and culinary skills. At only twenty-two, he was head chef at the restaurant, his specialties being soups, cheesecake, homemade ice cream, and an otherworldly cheese-and-walnut loaf that he prepared to the delight of us all. Even Dad commented how he didn't miss eating meat. It was actually the first time I'd gotten to taste it myself, as Source Family members didn't eat our restaurant food because it had been cut open for too long.

Mother knew I couldn't be happy in Chicago anymore. She saw how my new life had changed and improved me in ways she never could, and she could see how in love I was with Pythias. I'm still not sure how, but she convinced Dad that it would be better for me to return to LA. I think Dad was just happy to have her home with him and wanted to evade any further drama.

After three weeks, my parents gave me permission. I made myself a new, white linen wedding dress with long sleeves that puffed a little at the top and narrowed at the wrists. It had a vee neck trimmed with a thin, twisted gold cord that crisscrossed in front, then tied in the back. Mother bought me a gold Tiffany "slave" bracelet instead of a wedding ring. I think she might have been trying to say something here . . .

We were married in City Hall with little fanfare and flew back to LA a few days later. It had not been an act for either of us. In my teenage heart, he was the one for whom I'd journeyed to the Source in the first place. After all of the interference I faced with Mutte, I had thought Pythias was lost to me, but our reunion in Chicago finally gave us the opportunity to be together. We were truly in love, and I thought that was that. And it was, for a little while.

14

And Then There Were Five

Living with Mutte continued to be an incredible challenge. One day, Mutte burst into our room grinning from ear to ear spouting, "I'm pregnant," about a week after our return.

A knot clenched in my stomach; she would now have a reason to rank over me. Trying to be happy for her, I said, "How wonderful. You'll be a beautiful mother."

Pythias lit up, reaching out to embrace her. The fact that we had a piece of paper stating we were married made no difference. I felt like an outsider, and for all of our bonding, the seed of life had taken no hold in me.

Mutte's rapidly producing ricochet hormones overwhelmed me. I would walk into the room, and she would break into tears, pushing me out of the way to snuggle up by Pythias' side. Even though I was quite willing to share him, her bellicose nature could not handle the reality of it. Pythias only wanted to make her calm and ensure she had a peaceful pregnancy, so all his attention was diverted to her.

Others were also challenged in their multiple relationships. Ahom couldn't handle their relationship with Celest, and soon Father Yod reinstated the one-man-with-one-woman policy as a result. This rendered me a single woman again. So I moved back up in the attic to a small closet-like space. In a way, it was a relief, but it still broke my heart. Pythias felt bad and would come up to console me, but Mutte would track him down. She was pregnant with his child, and he was obligated to that child, not me.

I distracted myself by getting more shifts at the Source Restaurant;

it gave me an opportunity to have close encounters with Father Yod, which I took full advantage of, as we all did. I spent all my spare time listening to his wisdom—sometimes even when I was supposed to be working. Father was happy to see me whenever I popped in.

One day while upstairs of the Source on a break, Father and I found ourselves alone. This was not unusual, as people came and went upstairs all the time. We would talk with him about any problems we had, discuss things we might not understand or, as in my case, just come to hang on his every word. We all clustered around him to listen.

He was sitting in full lotus with his long silver and gold locks tumbling over his shoulders and a shawl wrapped around him. His back was to the altar, and he spoke of something he'd read in a book. "It's over in that stack," he said as he pointed across the room. "Would you fetch it for me?"

I recall wearing a long, white gown, in a lightweight T-shirt fabric, suspended from my shoulders by a lace yoke just above my breasts. Because the ceiling was very low in that corner of the room, I crawled over to retrieve the book. I moved slowly and deliberately, like a cat. What was I doing? It felt very sexy, and I took pleasure from it. I could feel his eyes following me, enjoying my grace. I scanned the stack, picked out the volume, turned, and caught his brilliant blue gaze while slowly returning.

He was mesmerized. Reaching for the book I was handing him, he brought me closer. I wedged into his lap, which was not unusual; he often gave us hugs seated that way. His hand touched my face, and I leaned in and nuzzled his soft, silver beard. I looked up, and our lips met. This was heaven. I dissolved in his embrace.

After a few minutes he asked, "Would you like to move in up here with me?"

"Yes, would I ever, Father!" My ears were zinging, along with every cell in my body!

"You can call me 'Yod,' now that we are to be lovers."

"But what about Ahom? She's your wife. Aren't the man and his woman one?"

"We are one, and I am also one with you."

He looked at me with tenderness as I accepted his resolve.

Father Yod & Me

Becoming his second woman was a bit controversial for the unenlightened on several levels. I was only seventeen, and he fifty-one. Ahom was five years older than me. As a precocious child, most people assumed I was older. The thing was, we were not relating to age, but to the soul. Age was an illusion. We all felt like we had been together in many different lifetimes.

In the early days of the Family, we all adhered to mono relationships: one man with one woman. There was no homosexuality; Yod did not view it as natural behavior for humans. As time went on, we began to experiment again, with men being with more than one woman. Today, it is oddly popular for others to look back on those times with revulsion. I don't equate what is going on in the twenty-first century to what transpired within the loving bonds of our dedicated Family. I stand by my experience and hold absolutely no regrets.

Ahom and I, fortunately, hit it off easily. She took me under her wing and made me feel welcome, like a little sister—so long as I remembered I was number two. And that was okay; I was just happy to be in his presence and share him. She, like Venus, was an older sister I never had. Plus,

Ahom and I shared similar features: long, curly, brown hair, brown eyes, and curvy figures—only she had tiny tits where mine were ample—and that Jewish DNA holding an invisible thread that bound us.

Ahom truly helped me feel comfortable in LA. As we hopped into Yod's yellow VW van, she proclaimed, "You need to have some nicer clothes as Yod's woman. I'm taking you shopping. We can go to the Swap Meet on Santa Monica and Granny Takes a Trip, and there are other small boutiques and thrift shops on Melrose." She flipped her hair over her shoulder and turned the key in the steering wheel.

She introduced me to the owners at International Silks and Woolens, where we indulged our mutual love of fabrics. Ahom often made dresses that became a style staple in the Family, and I admired that. A trip to the Bodhi Tree Bookstore was often our last stop on the way home. She was very generous and frequently bought me trinkets along with her own purchases.

I enjoyed my time with Yod and Ahom. She and I ventured to get along without stress, unlike the triad of Mutte, Pythias, and me. Venus observed this and wanted a part of it too. One day Ahom and I returned to find Venus had taken roost upstairs in our little apartment above the restaurant, smiling like a Cheshire Cat.

Now four, we adjusted for Venus. Soon along came Makushla, tall, solid, and serene. This pyramid went on for some time, a little juggling act for us all to find our places. Yod seemed amused. Once after meditation, he reflected, "Ahom, you are my wife; Bonadea, my child bride; Venus, you are my friend; and Makushla, you are my mother." These became the relationship archetypes that evolved. If it worked for Abraham to have four wives, it did for him.

We learned to be conscious of each other's space and to respect our space with Yod. It was all a very close fit up there. We had to. We would take turns at night: two of us massaging Yod, the other two massaging each other. We shared our energy and refined our duties. I became the one to comb his hair. His scalp was extremely sensitive, and his hair long and curly like mine. I deftly took the tangles out. Ahom mostly took charge of his food. Yod and Venus were often in intellectual pursuit, and Makushla made sure the rest of his bits and pieces were all organized. I was happy and comfortable with Ahom and Venus, and Makushla was a sweet soul who endeavored to make peace at every turn.

Our happy little pyramid lasted for several weeks until Isis burst in to challenge the status quo. Isis had been with Osiris but was always focused on Father, taking pictures and recording each morning class. He called her "the record keeper." If we were all with him, why couldn't she be? She wasn't going to miss out on anything! And Isis did not budge, holding the stone face of a Sphinx. He also called her his "hatchet woman" and sometimes "dragon lady." Yod felt that women should have a part in making a relationship and that if a woman approached a man, he should accept her. He felt it was fair.

Isis became the bull in the china shop. As we walked out together, she became obsessed, acting like his personal bodyguard and commanding everyone to be three feet away from him. She ruffled all our feathers, Yod included. We all stood back and watched on edge as she dove in and tried to push us around, saying it was all for Yod. Our harmonious little experiment had gone awry. She provoked us all, making our new relationship profoundly uncomfortable. A constant tension surrounded us.

She began to treat Yod as if he were Jesus. On the third day, she brought a seven-precious-metal bowl filled with water and laid it at his feet. Sensually she washed every inch of them, then attempted to dry them with her hair. That was the breaking point.

"Enough of this, Isis! I can't take any more!" Yod shouted. "All of you, I need you to leave. Take all your things; I need some space around here. You can all go to the Mother House!"

I had never heard him angry like that before and never would again. It only took her three days to break up our happy little scenario. Isis and I are close today, and I still try to get her to laugh about this.

15

Here Today, Gone to Maui

Makushla, Isis, and I dragged our feet to the Mother House, and Ahom to Source Arts, where some ex-Family members still lived. Ahom resented the whole thing blowing up as it did and in no way wanted to face Isis—or any of us for that matter. Venus made her way to the cash register, helped herself to $200, grabbed her sewing machine, and vanished to Maui.

We were bewildered and held hope for the dust to settle. Isis returned to Osiris, but Makushla and I both felt a bit lost. Yod needed time alone to air out from it all. It took about a week till he allowed us to be near—but not to live with him. Nonetheless, Ahom and Makushla eventually found their way back to him.

△ ▽ △ ▽

In the late winter of early 1973, the lease had run out on the Mother House. Our neighbors could not understand or put up with our lifestyle and complained to the owners, who then refused to renew.

On top of having to find a new LA home, a contingent led by Waterfall had been sent out to Maui to look for a settlement there. And then, to add to all of these other events, Mutte and Mushroom's mother began sending messages to the Source that she wanted her younger daughter home, and we all knew what she had done the last time. This time Yahowha was prepared: he did not even tell the Family what steps he was taking. Mushroom just disappeared one day, and no one said anything about it. We were all so wrapped up in the other elements of change that it was almost as if she may have run away.

The Father House was located in Nichols Canyon above Hollywood, and the Family began to pack up. It was much smaller than the Mother House but was nestled into the top of a hillside on Nichols Canyon Drive with an expansive view of the city and was also more private, with no neighbors.

In preparation for the move, Yod also felt it would be a good idea to get some of the women and children to Maui. Waterfall had procured a five-acre piece of land in Makawao that contained a couple of cabins, a garden, and a water line that sat between a fallow pineapple plantation and a guava orchard. He described it as heaven on earth. It would be easier to change homes and get the house fitted out if there were fewer people to move—plus, there was not enough room for everyone in the Father House.

Yod also thought it was time to move in with the Family, and one of the bedrooms was prepared for him. Makushla and Ahom would move in with him. He envisioned fitting everyone else in by building cubby holes just big enough for a sleeping pad, stacked on top of each other. In addition, a small pyramid tent on a platform was to be erected at the bottom of the hill, where Yod could get some privacy for meditation.

And then the sheriff's department showed up at the restaurant looking for Mushroom. Thankfully I was not there at the time, but Yod called the house to have me spirited away in case they showed up there. I was, after all, still underage, and he did not want to take a chance, even if I did hold a marriage license.

I was taken to an apartment in Hollywood under the shelter of Lotus Weinstock, who had left the Family some months before with her daughter Cherub. Lotus was a singer and comedian prior to the Family and was Lenny Bruce's last lover. We always got along well, so I felt comfortable with her. But I had no idea what was to come next. Lotus entertained me with stories of her life and what had been. She told me about someone breaking into her apartment one night and threatening to rape her. Telling him that Jesus would not be happy about that, she went on a spiritual tirade, informing him of the great sin he would be committing, bringing him to a puddle of tears on her bedroom floor. She was a beautiful, blue-eyed blonde with a wide, sexy smile, and the man could have overtaken her easily. But she was also a clever woman, and lucky. The angels had definitely been on her side.

I spent a night or two with Lotus till Yod came up with a plan. He arranged for plane tickets, and I was safely off to Maui in the blink of an eye before the sheriff had a chance to find me. It was also an answer to what to do with Bonadea after the scattering of his women.

Magical Maui

After my return from Chicago with Pythias, the heartbreak of pregnant Mutte elbowing me out of our relationship, and the upset of the crumbling of our pyramid upstairs of the Source with Yod, I was eager to go. Hawaii was a new adventure, even if I would miss him dearly. There was now an additional urgency to fly the children and underage women over to Maui. It was not just the backlash from Mutte and Mushroom's mom—another woman in the Family who had sought help at an emergency room when her baby had staph had raised suspicions of the authorities too. Maui became our haven from the LA Sheriffs' Department and hastened our mission to find a new home for the Family to avoid any of the coming catastrophes we believed were about to beset the world. The world was to tip on its axis, and waters were to rise and cover land, like most of California. These beliefs were based on the predictions of Nostradamus and the Great Pyramid.

Yod wanted to establish a home for the entire Family away from LA. He envisioned a geodesic dome community where we could live as well as operate a spa there where we could teach people how to lead healthier lives. There had already been a trial trip to Molokai, but that had not panned out for us. So it was off to Maui.

I had never been to Hawaii—something I'd fantasized about since meeting Michael "Numbnuts" Stewart in Chicago after he had returned from Maui in 1969. He had shared stories of camping on the beach, living in harmony with nature, and eating bananas, coconuts, and mangos from the trees.

I stared out the window while the plane descended, taking in the lush, green hills and little towns, and then the runway. But where was the airport? There were a few warehouse buildings at its end, but that was it. Kahului was still a small, sleepy town in 1973. After landing, I grabbed my carry-ons and gleefully descended down the plane's stairway to the tarmac, greeted by the aroma of a blend of dust and sea with a floral top note on the warm breeze. I inhaled deeply. This aroma stayed with me, and I still feel the same way whenever I land in Hawaii.

A line of passengers headed toward a warehouse, and I followed them through to the other side and out to the street. An old, white van with no windows but an open sliding side door revealed several women, children, and a couple of Suns waiting at the curbside to retrieve me. Yod called all the men his "sons" but spelled it S-u-n.

The driver grinned and said, "Aloha! Welcome to Maui. Hope you enjoyed your trip. Get ready for a surprise. Makawao is upcountry and an hour away. We still have errands to run, and picking you up is only one of them. So climb in."

I peeked in the van. There was a bench along one side, a few wooden crates, and some blankets with pillows. Every surface was occupied, so I squeezed onto a blanket on the floor with my small travel bag next to Soma. Taking in her wide, generous grin, I soon found her five-year-old daughter, Starwoman, in my lap, chattering on about life in the jungle. We wound our way over bumpy roads around Kahului to Paia, stopped at the health food store, and then headed up to our five acres in Makawao.

Soma and Starwoman asked me lots of questions along the way. "Who is with Father Yod now?" "What happened to the Mother House?" "Did you bring any class tapes?" I relayed news of what the Family had been up to in LA, but mostly everyone was excited to hear about the latest tapes.

Soma explained, "In the mornings, meditation is in our kitchen or around the campfire if it's not raining. We listen to the tapes sent from class in LA."

I learned that the five-acre property in upper Makawao had been rented from a man named Winston. Finally, we turned onto the long driveway running beside a garden that curved into a green cluster of trees. Soma began a running commentary as we slowly drove by different parts of the camp on an unpaved bumpy driveway. "I live in that treehouse over there. It's for the women and children and is made of old windows and doors. Waterfall built it. The men built all the other treehouses, those tents on platforms, and those huts with screened wood framing and tin roofs."

I asked, "Where does the water come from?"

She pointed towards the front of the land. "A water line runs from the road onto the property. We hooked up a flush toilet in that small outhouse. The hose on the outside of it goes over to the laundry." Several large, galvanized wash tubs were set up on a level bed of rocks below the outhouse and next to the shower, which was a pallet platform with four posts and heavy plastic sheeting stapled around it. "We use the same hose for both the showers and wash tubs."

"Okay," I thought. "I guess I can adapt to this new adventure!"

The van slowly rolled to a stop beside an open-air kitchen with a gravel floor beneath a rustic wood cabin on long legs. Provisions were unloaded. There was no refrigerator. There was no electricity. There was a large cooler with big bags of ice to keep the milk cold. It was all flashlights and batteries from here on out. A long wood table with a sink built into it extended down the left side, a picnic table in the center, and on the right, some tall cabinets with screened doors to keep the critters and bugs out. A fire pit filled with ash in a circle of lava rocks sat twenty feet away in the open.

I met a few new Family members and reunited with familiar ones, and was pleasantly surprised to find Venus smiling at my entrance. Ramacharaka (James from Chicago) was with Mushroom and gave me a warm embrace, helping me feel at ease. Hypatia and her son Axis ran up. She had joined the Family a few days after me, and we had gotten close after it became my duty to teach the children at the Mother House—really more like babysitting. I loved these kids, and a flock of them jumped for joy to see me, climbing up me like spiders as they gave me a group hug.

"Where are the bathrooms?" I asked.

"Bonadea! Bonadea! Come with me! I'll show you," Starwoman, their ringleader, screeched as she grabbed my hand to lead me along with the small herd to their flush toilet in the outhouse. They noisily waited outside by the washtubs. Children can adapt to anything. This was all so rustic, but what did I expect? We had lived in the lap of luxury in LA. Here, it was back to the nature we idealized—except for the red mud that left its trace on everything.

"Where am I staying, Starwoman?"

"Just over there!" And she pointed to a tent on a platform where Heaven sat with Sol Amon on its steps. Grabbing my hand once again, she pulled me over to the plywood platform two feet off the ground with three wide, wooden stairs leading up to it. The children swarmed together and sat down while I got settled in my tent bedroom. Sol Amon reached for me to hold him, but Heaven seemed a bit reserved as she pointed out my sleeping spot on the other side—only inches from them. It seemed the camp was so tight for space that I was to sleep on the floor next to Heaven and Sunflower, Sol Amon's parents.

"Now let me show you our treehouse," blurted Starwoman. This time I reached my hand out, ready. We all ran to the treehouse built on multi-level wood platforms in a towering, aged eucalyptus tree that was enclosed using scavenged old windows and doors. The kids led me up several levels of the tour until we found Venus's space at the top.

The children dispersed for a snack, and Venus took me for a walk down the hill behind our camp to what was to become my Maui happy place, a waterfall and its pond surrounded by room-sized boulders. I felt a wave of relief that all was well after our traumatic split above the Source. She didn't bring it up at all, nor did I wish to.

We waded in, and I watched Venus swim over to the spot where the water cascaded from a stream, over the boulders, and into the pond. She swam under the flowing water that splashed over her head in a strong current. I followed. "I have to feel that too. It looks so refreshing!" When I close my eyes, I can still feel the heavy, soothing water pounding on my scalp and cleansing every inch of my being as it rushes over me. Now the initiation was complete. I was one with the land and ready for this new chapter of my Source Family adventure.

Everyone in our camp was living in very tight quarters and sleeping side by side. There were about thirty of us in total. It became virtually impossible to keep all our white clothes spotless while living in the red dirt! The lack of bleach and hot water meant we couldn't keep them clean, which resulted in our straying to different colors. It was the same for hemlines: floor-length frocks didn't weather well being dragged through the mud.

On one side of our property were several acres of wire-fenced guava orchard. Cows often roamed through them looking for fallen fruit and leaving behind their treasured cowpies. Treasured because of what grew from them: magic psilocybin mushrooms!

On the other side was an abandoned pineapple plantation filled with wild, sweet, but acidic fruit. Since we ate what we could grow or pick, that meant a lot of coconuts, and when in season, breadfruit, avocados, bananas, papayas, and mangos. At this moment the abundance was pineapple. Have you ever heard of pineapple mouth? The corners of your mouth get raw and crusty with sores from eating too much of the fruit. The acid does what acid does and eats away at your skin.

Coconut had never been to my liking, as I had only experienced the sweetened, flaked sort used for baking. But fresh coconut out of the shell is nothing like it. The mature hard meat has a satisfying moist crunch, and the soft meat from the younger coconuts can be whipped up and made into a sort of cream. Guavas became an acquired taste for me. They were sweet but tart and filled with hard, little seeds that were difficult to pick from my teeth. You also had to squeeze them open first to make sure they were not filled with tiny worms.

Breadfruit was versatile. It could be eaten ripe or green. Cooked, they filled you up with a hearty, soft texture like dense bread. We did not eat them ripe. We would toss them green into the fire pit and take out after an hour, cutting them open and scooping out the flesh. If we were lucky and had some butter, that was a real treat, but avocado was a pleasing addition too.

Mango season was my favorite. Sitting on the steps of our tent site with a colander mounded with them, Heaven, Sol Amon, and I would be in total bliss, with mango juice dripping from our fingers, the corners of our mouths, and over the edge of the steps into the dirt. Afterward, we went down to the waterfall to wash the whole mess off!

Sunflower became almost skeletal at one point. Nothing he ate would stick to his bones. The rest of us were pretty slim, but not like him. We had so little money, and what we did have was used to pick up a few meager provisions in town. On one of our outings, someone discovered him buying a small bag of dates and chastised him for it. I stood up for him, saying, "If he's going to work hard to provide for us all, he needs to be better nourished." He smiled back hearing this. My feelings for him had kindled.

Father thought it was a good exercise for us to see if we could fend for ourselves. And since much money was being spent on the new Father House in LA, we received only a meager financial infusion from the mainland. So the men had to work odd jobs doing carpentry or whatever they could find to help provide for all the women and children. We needed to buy things like toilet paper, soap, coffee, tea, and whatever extras that money afforded. At the front of the property was a large garden filled with greens, tomatoes, and herbs, and we were all required to put in some time there, usually in the morning when the sun wasn't so strong. Each afternoon was spent at the waterfall, washing off the dirt, lying on the boulders in the warm sun, and sharing our dreams.

△ ▽ △ ▽

Yod and Makushla came to visit for several days after he took her back to be with him. Ahom was not too happy about it, but Makushla was thrilled to be in Hawaii for the first time and overjoyed to have a little space with him to herself. We were over the moon to show Yod what we had made of our little slice of heaven, and we all missed his presence dearly.

"Look at what I've brought you," Father said as a couple of Suns lifted a fifty-gallon cardboard barrel out of the van along with their bags. "I didn't want you to think I wasn't hearing your complaints of starvation. Dr. Bronner's mineral salt has a compound formula of natural vitamins, minerals, seasonings, and sea vegetables. It'll make a healthy addition to your diet."

We were so grateful for this tasty nutritional supplement and we sprinkled it on everything: salads, avocado, and my favorite, coconut. Hypatia hugged him and asked, "Did you know you sent us to live like this?" He paused for a bit, looked around as he held her, and took it all in as he responded, "No. But one day, you'll look back on this as one of the best times of your life." I may not think of those Maui moments as the time of my life, but they were spectacularly special.

Father Yod and Makushla slept in a tent while there, and she said it was like the Garden of Eden, with all the ripe bounty to be eaten right from our land. In fact, she experienced a magical transition at the waterfall. Having arrived on Maui with a bladder infection, she found herself cured after swimming there.

I was hardly able to connect with Father Yod at all. Feeling like the rest of our little tribe that we had not been around him for a long time, I kept in the background. We did have a swim together in the pond, but there was a distance between us, and I could not account for it. He was first and foremost my earthly, spiritual Father, so I accepted and trusted whatever was to be. I found myself more focused on Sunflower after they left.

△ ▽ △ ▽

The Suns had discovered a restaurant in Paia Town on the main street that had been operating as "Charley's" and was going downhill. We needed a business to help generate funds. Sunflower was there one day when someone yelled out in frustration, asking if anyone knew how to cook. He seized his opportunity and stepped in. Eventually, an arrangement was made, and we took over to create the Source Paia. Waterfall became the head chef, but after my encounter with him when I had first landed at the Source, I made it my business to stay as far from him as possible.

The building had an old, wooden Western style front—it had been a theater in the past. Off the front was the old ticket booth with a window to the main street of town. We created smoothies and sold ready-made sandwiches from that window. I worked from the window a few days a week and enjoyed making the food and growing alfalfa sprouts in jars on a small shelf next to the fridge. Sometimes people would bring in magic mushrooms, requesting they be added to their food, and we happily obliged. Inside was a spacious dining room and full kitchen hosting a regular menu. This was where Waterfall was inspired to create a popular dish called the Magic Mushroom, which was added to the Source menu in LA. It was a pile of sautéed seaweed, mushrooms, bean sprouts, and onions, seasoned with shoyu and sesame oil, served over a bed of brown rice and topped with cheddar cheese and sometimes a scoop of cottage cheese. The mushrooms were now button mushrooms.

16

Paradise Lost, Dreaming Anew

Magic mushrooms grew abundantly on the island, as there were many cattle farms. It was a well-known fact they grew from cowpies, and they became a cheap and preferred drug of choice for the hippie population. Since they were so close at hand, we also experienced them.

There was a scary incident, though. The children crossed the fence of the guava patch and consumed a bunch of wild mushrooms from the cowpies. They were their own little tribe, always watching out for each other and playing all over the property. I was sitting on the steps of my tent when I heard screaming and kids shouting and raced to find the children climbing like monkeys in the guava trees, screeching at each other. Many of the other adults came running. Each of the children was lovingly picked up by their parents, who attempted to calm them down. Axis and Starwoman had gone feral, and shrieking of spiders, the plastic sheeting around the shower, what was lurking in the guava orchard, and who knows what else was upsetting their fragile psyches. I had to step away while watching their parents talking the children down; some were still upset and needed several hours to come down from it. The parents decided a closer eye must be kept on the children and that they were not to be allowed access to the guava patch unescorted. Mushrooms always made me laugh; I couldn't imagine what had turned their little heads around.

△ ▽ △ ▽

My stint at the restaurant in Paia came to an abrupt halt when I came down with a case of scabies. Who knows where it came from? They nested in between my fingers and itched like crazy, especially at night. I started to have unstoppable itching episodes no amount of calamine lotion could appease. At one point, it brought me to tears. I had no idea what was going on at first. Sunflower didn't know what it was, and neither did most of the others. We were all middle-class kids and had no experience with it. Then most everyone got it. It rattled my nerves, and some even became resentful that I had caught and spread it. Some hippies in town filled us in on what it was. We then went through the nightmare of having to launder *everything*. Every single piece of fabric had to be washed, then taken to town and put in the big dryers to kill the mites. Quell lotion was spread on our skin to kill them; we could not solve this with natural substances. I had never experienced anything like it in my life. It still puts shivers down my spine.

Soon after we healed from that, Father Yod brought Sunflower back to LA. Yod was putting a band together, and Sunflower was to be his bass player. He also needed Sunflower's help and expertise to move the Family into the Father House. Little by little we all returned. It was hard leaving our slice of paradise, but after being run ragged from the trials of mud, lack of food, lack of funds, scabies, and most of all, not being around Father Yod, we were ready to go. We survived this rugged life in as positive a mind frame as possible, trying to adapt to our surroundings. I have to admit, I was happy to be returning to LA.

Venus, Harvest Moon, and I were to travel together. On our last day, Venus and I woke up and packed our few possessions, and Venus said, "Let's go out and walk the land for the last time. As we're taking the red eye back to LA there's plenty of time." She carried a Mason jar filled with coffee, and we headed down a path through the guava patch. There were plenty of cowpies brimming with mushrooms. We thought it would be fun to fly out in classic Maui style and began consuming them. Venus finished her coffee and said, "There are so many today. Maybe we should gather some to take with us. It would be a shame to waste." We carefully nipped the stems above the cowpies, dropped them in the jar, and proceeded to eat one then stash one, as we wound our way down the hill into the jungle and onto the little valley floor.

We continued on the trail of mushrooms till we were so deep in the forest that the light dimmed. The mushrooms began taking hold. I had no idea of the amount we had consumed and really didn't care. The experience was so beautiful; how could they hurt me? I felt completely in tune with the nature around me. We came to a place where two trees had fallen down ten feet apart and sat down opposite each other.

Venus whispered, "Sit still, don't move, and just look into my eyes." She looked back into mine. From the sides of our eyes, the forest came alive. All the trees, ferns, and foliage were breathing. We watched as they inhaled and exhaled. A green, earthy scent filled our lungs. Invisible beings emerged and flitted about so fast it was impossible to focus on them. We became truly one with the moment and the forest. Our surroundings welcomed us as if we were expected and they were putting on a final show for us.

We sat for some time, staring into each other's eyes and glimpsing the animation from our peripheral vision. The beauty of the experience kept us smiling. That's the thing about mushrooms. They can get you into a happy space and take you away. You find the humor in everything, making it easy to smile about it all. You realize what a tiny piece of this puzzle of life you are. I am sure that when the children took them, they did not know how to transpose those thoughts because they were too young to see the dichotomies and laugh.

The moment arrived, and we knew it was time to go. Venus picked up the now-full Mason jar, and we trailed out of the forest, strolling along the little stream that led to the waterfall. We dipped in for our final baptism—a full circle from my first day in Maui.

I lay down on the giant boulder in the sun for one last time, reflecting on my Maui adventures. It had been only a few, short months but felt much longer. I had never experienced living in a tent, hardly having food or money, washing clothes by hand in a tub sitting on rocks, or taking cold, outdoor showers on rainy days. It had built inner strength, the kind you earn when you survive some trauma and turn it around. I could do anything now. Maui taught me things I still hold to today: being self-reliant, resourceful, and patient. After the sun dried us, we hiked back up the hill to our camp and found everyone in a quandary about what had happened to us.

Harvest, stared at the jar and asked, "What are you going to do with all those mushrooms?"

Venus joyfully replied, "We picked them to take back for the Family."

"How are you going to do that?" she asked.

"Hmm. I haven't thought that far yet," said Venus.

In those days, they did not search your luggage or your body, but there was always the rule that you could not bring fresh fruits or vegetables on the plane.

Harvest lit up with an idea, and said, "Let's make some avo sandwiches for the plane and pile the mushrooms in them."

So we busied ourselves making sandwiches to bring with us on the plane. In those days, they served meals on flights that we would never dream of eating. We could remove the layer of mushrooms as we ate, to save.

We arrived at the airport, checked our bags, and headed to the agricultural inspection.

"What's in the paper bags?" the inspector queried with authority.

"Just some avocado sandwiches for the flight. We don't eat the kind of food the plane serves," Harvest replied.

"You say there's avocado in those sandwiches? You can't bring avocados on the plane, you know. They're *kapu*, forbidden," stated the inspector, straightening up with even more authority. "I can throw them away for you if you'd like?"

"No, no, that's okay," Harvest answered. "We'll eat them before going through."

We turned around, walked back to the area near the sidewalk entrance, and stood there devouring the sandwiches. I was still a little high from that morning's adventures, so this soon put me right back where I had started. It's a good thing that you can just follow the crowd in the airport and act like you know what you are doing because we were flying higher than the plane was that day!

17

New Era LA: The Father House

Venus, Harvest Moon, and I returned from Maui to be picked up by a familiar red and white VW van and driven to our new Father House. We rode up a long, steep, winding driveway into the hills of Hollywood, to a plateau-like open space. A wide, paved expanse fronted the home, and a small, gravel parking area nestled next to the ochre canyon wall. A large, white two-story house trimmed in yellow peeked over a panoramic vista of the entire city of LA. A pool sat between the garage and canyon wall enclosed by a simple, black, wrought-iron fence. There was no grass or garden area, only a few bushes and trees. The dusty canyon smelled of sage, with its sparse growth dotting the hillside above. In contrast, the hillside below us was verdant.

Several Family members were sprawled around the kidney-shaped pool, which included a hot tub. Someone was standing under the outdoor shower mounted off the garage wall. A roomy, cement patio surrounded the pool, furnished with wooden massage tables and naked people giving and receiving massages. A few lounge chairs and a built-in, round cement table with an umbrella and benches were filled with other Family members and children relaxing or at play. When our Volkswagen van rolled up, everyone looked to see who had arrived.

"Bonadea!" screamed a brigade of young, naked children who raced out to embrace me as I stepped out of the van. They had come home a few weeks earlier. Those kids did miss me—I was closer to their age, a big sister. Everyone wanted to know what had happened in

Maui, and to be honest, I was still feeling the effects of the magic mushrooms we had consumed before getting on the plane! This all still felt quite surreal. Venus and Harvest had already ventured into the house, and I just wanted to get settled but was happy to see the children. "I'll catch up with you guys later," I assured them and headed to the front door, anxious about our new home. Sister Rain greeted me with a warm hug as the door opened.

"It's so good to have you home, Bonadea. I can give you a tour of our new house if you want?"

"Yes, I'd love that, but can you tell me where I'm staying? I'm beat," I replied, feeling relieved. Rain was an Angel and a completely free spirit with a jovial sense of humor. She and I felt a particular kinship for each other. Tall with wild, frizzy, shoulder-length dark hair and large, laughing, brown eyes, her company relaxed me as she led me on a tour.

I followed her past a staircase on the left viewing a large living room in front of us. A floor-to-ceiling picture window overlooked the city at the opposite end of the room, "This is our new meditation room," she beamed. The familiar smell of our Family's favorite sandalwood incense from the Vedanta society scented the air. I had missed that.

"There's a powder room tucked under the stairs and a dining room off the right, which holds the overflow of people for class in the morning." There was nothing but a wool rug on the floor. Noticing my look of confusion she added, "We either eat outside or cross-legged on the floor."

"What's behind the glass doors across the room?" I asked.

"I guess it must have been an office, den, or library, with all those tall, wooden bookcases. But we use it as living quarters. I think about five people are living in there," she said.

We walked through a doorway beside the dining room. "This is where the children all live together," she said, and we stepped into a large, long room gaily decorated with learning materials of letters, numbers, and symbols in bright colors surrounding children's artwork. A fireplace sat at the base of the far rock wall. They also had their own full bathroom. We moved on to the kitchen off of the dining room. The generous food preparation area overlooked the canyon's city views, with broad counters, white cupboards, and a separate pantry filled with jars of herbs and spices. A back door led out to the garage, industrial laundry machines, and pool. Rain stood by a large, wooden shelf unit propped against the garage, the kind of thing you would see at a market with its shelves tilted up in the back to showcase its wares. "Joshua stocks our produce here." It was filled with boxes of fresh melons, onions, apples, broccoli, and various fruits and vegetables that did not need refrigeration. The cooler air at that elevation was enough to preserve it.

"I'll bet you're ready to see the cubby holes!"

Our construction crew had built honeycomb-like cubby holes throughout the house. Each one was a 4X4X8-foot space. Rain explained, "If you are a couple, a sliding wood panel can be removed from between, allowing a double space."

We found rows of these constructed two high in several rooms upstairs. "If you're really committed, you can stay in the same place for a while." (Our relationships were often fluid). "There aren't enough cubbies for everyone, so some of the single men have built little tent-like structures on platforms on the lower hillside."

At the top of the second-floor stairs were two closed bedroom doors, and the next room had a large ensuite bathroom. "This is Father's bedroom." She pointed to one of the closed doors. "But he hasn't moved in yet. The other is a small room with four cubbies." We stepped further into the next room, which was dominated by six cubby holes. It was kind of sparse, but the cubbies looked neat with their tidy beds—some with little curtains hanging at the ends for privacy. Everyone must have been at the pool.

I spied one unoccupied next to a window abutting Yod's bedroom. "Bonadea, you can have the cubby on the end there," she said.

"I was hoping you would say that," I said as I left the bag I was carrying in the open space and followed Rain to finish the tour as she pointed up.

"Up there is the trap door to the attic." She reached up and pulled down a wooden, accordion, ladder-like stairway for us to ascend. The attic spanned the length of the house, its floor fully carpeted. Fabric was stapled over the slanting roof beams to finish the room, which draped straight down about three feet from the floor to offer storage space behind. It was very much like the little space Yod had over the Source. If one slept in the attic, bedding needed to be stowed because everyone slept almost side by side, kind of like it was in Maui.

We traversed back down and through the next doorway to find a wide, long room with windows all around lit by the sun. Many duplex cubbies were built here, six on the right and then maybe sixteen along the entire length of the left wall, with another two just at the top of the stairs leading back down to the kitchen. "This one's mine." Rain motioned to a cubby with a velvet blanket and a little altar set at the back with a triangle mirror and candles. Lace hung across the ceiling, giving it a cozy feel.

A few steps down to the end of the row, she brightened as she said, "And here's our closet. We all share our clothes now." A ten-foot wooden dowel fastened on one side of the two cubbies at the top of the stairs was stretched over to the opposite wall, and the women's dresses were hanging there.

"Wow, this is a far cry from our spacious, vintage Mother House. But after living in the jungle, I'm happy to have hot water on tap, no more red mud, and a bed without bugs," I said. I wasn't so sure about sharing clothes, but oh well! I kept that to myself.

In front of Father House Garage; Odin, Galaxy, Damascus, Heaven, Justice

Music for Our Souls

The music had begun to come together while we were in Maui. Octavius, a professional drummer, had joined the Family. Djin and Pythias were on guitars, and Sunflower on bass, so Yod now had a full band.

One day, Yod asked for Octavius to come see him. "Sun, I need you to transform the garage into a music studio. Purchase everything you need, including soundproofing, instruments, and recording equipment." He wanted to give his Suns more creative output, and we couldn't help but soak up the energy of the times: sex, drugs, and rock 'n' roll. Octavius built a glassed-in sound booth, plus a larger open space for the band to play in. He lined the walls in foam and draped them with thick, elegant fabrics. Persian rugs were spread on the floors. After class, they would all end up in the band room rolling out new tunes. As many of the Family that could squeeze in would huddle against the wall in the band room abutting the sound booth. There usually was not enough room for everyone, so Yod had some speakers set up in the meditation room, allowing everyone to hear what was coming down. The musicians would play their songs, eventually leading to improvisational jam sessions.

The improvs usually started out with Octavius laying down a beat on drums with Sunflower chiming in on bass. Sometimes using a violin bow or a feather, Djin elicited as many different sounds as he could from his guitar. Strumming a steady stream on his Flying V rhythm guitar was Pythias, and Rhythm or Vibration often keyed a melody on the Leslie organ. Yod became inspired to join them on a large, copper kettle drum.

He had his own way with the kettle drum and began coming down with lyrics spontaneously, the band following suit with the music. Just as he did in class, it started out in the breath—silent, sometimes chanting—then the musical tones seeped in, and Yod's words would begin coming down. Zinuru recorded every note in the sound booth. With the profits from the restaurant and additional help from our patron saint of money, Damascus, several different albums were pressed.

This would be a new way for us to get Yod's word out. We placed them on sale in the little shop next to the restaurant and also sent representatives to shop the big record companies but were turned down. The music was too avant-garde for the mainstream music companies. So we decided to do it on our own, and Higher Key Records was born. Today it's known as psychedelic rock, and the records have become popular collectors' items, some selling for thousands.

18

Becoming One

At three in the morning, it would be dark, quiet, and the world still. Yod would ask, "Have you ever noticed that if you stay up late after midnight, you feel a second wind? That is when universal life energy revs itself back up and waxes as the day builds."

While the giant metropolis of LA was asleep, we would awake to a hive of silent activity. Waking up with 140 people could be a traffic jam, but we would become acutely aware of each other's movements. Someone, usually a soft-spoken person, would circulate around the sleeping areas, quietly speaking, "Yahowha, time to rise and shine," to anyone not yet awake. It took time to get used to this, but eventually, an inner alarm clock would kick in.

Yod, a big fan of physical fitness, prescribed exercise as the first thing to do when we awoke. My routine usually began out by our pool, with a few jump squats and additional calisthenics and stretches, followed by some laps. At that hour the pool was briskly cold, but another of his other prescriptions was taking a cold shower in the morning to cleanse our body of any negative energy attached during sleep. So I would jump into the cold pool, and that counted. Plus, I didn't have much company at that hour; it was strictly for the brave. I would then luxuriate in a two-minute warm shower after my swim in the pool's outdoor shower—less traffic than the bathrooms inside.

It is still a marvel to me how we were all able to accomplish this so cheerfully and respectfully of each other. Our aim was to be kind and positive to all mind, energy, and matter. It was not easy learning to live together in this hive-like atmosphere. Everyone was on a different schedule. Some worked during the day, others at night. The only time we were all together was during our early morning meditation. Some had a hard time learning to control themselves while moving around quietly. One morning Yod said, "Move like a mouse creeping through the house or a thief in the night. There is nothing that you have to say that can't be held till you get downstairs, so as not to disturb anyone behind their curtain. Stop this shit of carrying your old habits with you. You must live for others and be considerate of them. You have nothing to fear."

I loved our morning rituals; they invigorated and provided purpose and a healthy start to the day. After toweling off, I took one minute at the sink to brush my teeth, then returned to my cubby to dress and brush my hair.

I often sneaked one of my own dresses from the communal closet the night before for the following morning. The clothes I had made were quite popular. Unfortunately, my dimensions were a bit bustier and wider in the hips, and sometimes only the smaller sizes were left by the time I got there. My favorite dresses were often ruined with holes from safety pins or vigorous laundering.

Then it was downstairs to set up my spot in the candle-lit meditation room. No one had a permanent spot to sit but Yod. He would sit in the lotus position nearest the window of the room on a small bench layered with blankets and sheepskins. A fifty-inch gong hung from a tubular steel stand behind his bench, which Yod would often use during our meditations to, as he would say, "get us out of ourselves." The early birds got to sit closest to him, and I wanted to sit as near as possible to absorb everything he was about to lay on us. After setting up my spot on the oversized, carved wool rug with a small blanket and pillow, I would make my way to the kitchen to get a cup of coffee dispensed from a catering-sized urn and then head back to my spot to prepare for meditation.

We would then practice breathing exercises or read if one sat near the candlelight. Eventually, someone started softly chanting, and all would join in. We chanted the Hebrew letters of the name of God, *Yod He Vau He,* and the name itself, Yahowha (pronounced *Yah-ho-whah*).

Yod would emerge around 4 a.m., deftly stepping around all the bodies sitting close in the lotus position through the flickering candlelight. The scent of sandalwood would waft around us, stirring the air with enchantment. What was going to come down today? People would lean out of the way for him to pass on his way to be seated in front of the gong and velvet-draped picture window. Makushla would then hand him his perfect cup of coffee. We only drank one cup of this a day, too much caffeine being unhealthy.

Sometimes we held a Sacred Herb (marijuana) ceremony before class. Someone prepared a pipe, and a line would form in front of them. We inhaled a six-second hit and returned back to our seats to hold it for as long as possible. That was all we needed to ignite us for what was to come.

Starwoman lying in my lap after meditation one morning.

Yod would say, "Thoth the Atlantean stated, 'The grass of the Arabs did not give me the light, I had that afore time, but so much insight I could not receive in ten lifetimes.'" We partook of marijuana as a sacred herb and treated it with great respect.

Our chanting continued together, Yod passionately leading us. Chanting together was like a flock of birds gathering to launch in formation. We synchronized our souls in union, preparing to ascend. It allowed us to get in tune with each other. He would start the chant, and after the first note, the rest of us chimed in, intuitively knowing the exact melody, tone, pitch, and cadence. This would continue for several minutes till he was inspired to change the tune.

There was a moment when intuitively we all became one. It was like being propelled up to the clouds to hover, then floating in the glow of it. Yod would then begin to "come down" as we called it, with the cosmic wisdom from the Akashic records he had tapped into. This is now known as channeling. Yod dove deep to find the answers to our cosmic quests, and the answers would flow—not with altered personalities, but with passion and love, like an a-ha moment. They were the answers to our questions—some of which we didn't even realize we were asking. Someone in the room would often expound, "Shew," an oral exclamation mark to getting it.

Being right there with him on that astral plane, seeking the knowledge and the excitement of finding the answers, was awesome. Mabel Collins wrote of traveling to the Halls of Amante, a cosmic library where the answers appeared written on the walls in her books *Light on the Path* and *Through the Gates of Gold*. Yod resonated with this and learned how to read those words, reflecting them back to us on how to live consciously conscious of the effects of our causes, or as mundane as how to properly fold sheets and towels! And laughter was always welcomed. Yod would find humor in everything. He saw the awkwardness in the truth and often broke out in song, at which point, we would join in, singing a tune from an old vaudeville act recalled from his childhood. "Are ya havin' any fun? Whatchya gettin' outta livin'? What good is what you got, if yer not, havin' any fun?"

On Sundays, we sometimes rented a projector, screen, and most often an old black-and-white film from one of the Hollywood film libraries. Yod loved watching old movies from the thirties and forties, and we loved watching them with him. The meditation room floor would fill with bodies lying side by side in front of the screen set by the window. Some of the melodies of our chants came from films, like the Exodus song from *The Bible*, and the theme song from *Bell, Book, and Candle*. The Hebrew National Anthem was another favorite. Yod was inspired by the melodies and chanted Yod He Vau He or Yahowha to them.

As the light outside began to rise, he waxed into stories of his life, experiences he had, and what he learned from them. If we had visitors, he acknowledged them and talked about why they had come and what they were seeking. At sunrise, we filed out the front door to greet it with the Star exercise. Facing the east, we tried to keep our eyes open to take in the seeping light as it peeked out from the horizon.

After sunrise, we returned to the meditation room to conquer the everyday dealings with our lives. Problems were solved, and questions answered. Yod would handle each one with respect and grace, not judging, only sorting things out. The restaurant crew soon would need to leave to open for breakfast. Those that stayed were usually treated to a session from the band, with Yod joining them.

19

Source Family Style

When I first became a member in 1972, everyone in the Family wore white, the reflection of all colors and purity. You need to be especially conscious of wearing white all the time because it gets dirty so quickly; thus, it was an exercise in awareness. We used various shades of white: ivory, natural, cream, and bright white. I liked natural even if it was harder to clean because it could not be bleached. Many of our clothes were acquired from the swap meets on Santa Monica Boulevard or second-hand stores in Hollywood. Women's old petticoat skirts were popular. Long and white, they tied at the waist with many tiers, ruffles, lace, and eyelets. Mexican muslin blouses and dresses with colorful embroidery were attractive back then and deemed acceptable. Yoga pants had not been invented; however, karate pants had. Made from dense woven-cotton sackcloth, they were loose fitting with a drawstring waist and maybe some pockets. Women did not wear trousers, but it seemed that men soon began wearing dresses!

Plans changed often in the Family. We adapted to the "energies" that "came down." Every day was a new adventure, and Father often said, "We live a year in a day." Sometimes we would be turning our ship around in midstream to chart a new direction! It helped us learn to be spontaneous and adaptable to the situation at hand. It taught us to laugh at ourselves and the temporary nature of all things and plans. It was also expensive, and we made plenty of mistakes trying to figure out the right plan for our unwieldy extended family.

As he transitioned from being called Father Yod to Yahowha, he took up wearing robes. They were more comfortable to wear while meditating and less restricting. Restrictive clothing keeps the body from breathing and performing its proper functions—exactly why we didn't wear underwear. The robes were not a bathrobe style, more like a long pullover top. The men felt uncomfortable wearing lighter-weight fabrics like those the women wore, so we constructed them of a heavier material, experimenting with velour, upholstery velvet, and terry cloth until we discovered homespun, which became our favorite. A simple weave, of soft thick heavy cotton, in white or natural that looked biblical, it had a nubby hand once washed. Its width was over five feet, so you got a lot for your yardage. The Homespun Company produced it originally for draperies. We fashioned robes, dresses, shawls, bags, bedspreads, and anything else we needed from it.

I fondly recall helping Soma make a dress one day. She spread the folded fabric on the floor, laid down on top of it, and said, "Bonadea, can you take this chalk and trace my body outline on the cloth?" I traced around her figure with her arms and legs spread out to the sides like a star. She took back the chalk and shaped long bell sleeves and a wide-swept hem, then cut it out, leaving room for seams. She sewed it together and put it on for a perfect fit! Soma, the Aquarian name for the moon, was a dancing star.

Father Yod observed my talents and encouraged me to sew Family-style clothes. They were inspired by designs reflecting ages past, like ancient Greek-era gowns, Renaissance and Victorian clothes, and of course, biblical vestments. I constructed many pieces and helped anyone who asked. I also made robes for Yod and a few lucky Suns.

Then Yod decided we should all pool our clothes in two big closets, men's and women's, and when we went to dress, we were to just go to the closet and pick something out. Theoretically, this was a way that no one became attached or was denied something nice to wear. But it didn't take into account size. Our clothes were made short or tall, thin or curvy, so they degraded from safety-pin holes and being dragged through the dirt. In some ways, we all broke these rules. I know I did, sneaking a dress the night before or hiding one I had made to preserve it! Essentially, this experiment did not last long.

At the Father House, the band went into the studio every day after class and became very comfortable playing spontaneous music together with Father. As this was all recorded, Father decided to make albums out of several of the tapes. *Kohoutek* became the first, instigated by the comet that was traveling near the earth at that time, March 7, 1973. I was still in Maui when this occurred so only received this news in the morning class tapes sent later on.

"When you receive a new name, it's because you are that or it's something you need to grow into," Father would say. One morning it came down that he was evolving from Yod. All the changes from moving to the Father House, sending part of the Family to Maui, and developing the band to become a focusing energy for the teachings to be dispensed were changing the way the Family was operating. We were evolving. In his aspiration to be more godlike and dispense with his personality, he took the name Yahowha. His aim was to be the word he was coming down with and constantly reflect that. Some thought he gave himself the name of God because he thought he was. He never said he was *the* god. He often said, "Man, you are god, not a horse's ass," "God created man in his image!" or "God is the little voice in the silence within. We all have God within us."

The music was a way for him to process what he was coming down with in a physical way, kind of like primal therapy. In the sixties, music and dance became more free form, and through moving to the music and singing, the bonds of conformity were shaken loose. Another facet of Yod's transition to Yahowha was the band name, which changed from Father Yod and the Spirit of '76 to Yahowha 13.

While there were a few who actually did view him as God incarnate, I took him at his word. I can understand why they thought that, having been raised as Christians and expecting Jesus to rise. I was raised Jewish. I knew Jesus only as one of us. He was a man in God's image who strove to be the best person he could be on this earth. I observed this in Yahowha. He never lied or deceived us. I'm sure there may have been a few omissions, but it was not to hide anything on purpose or to deceive, it was more like the results of an experiment in living that did not pan out well. Honesty radiated from his eyes.

One morning in the band room while they were recording the *Expansion* and *Contraction* albums, a bunch of us sat huddled on the floor next to Yahowha talking. At that point, I had attempted to be in relationships with his Suns, but nothing was working out. I just wanted to be around him. I seized my opportunity to ask him, "Lately, I've been thinking the name Bonadea is keeping me that priestess in the ivory tower. Do you think I could benefit from changing my name?"

Yahowha looked at me with an expression I had craved for a long time, one of adoration and appreciation. It was not just the way he looked at all his Suns and Daughters, but the way he looked at me when he loved what I was doing. He shut his eyes for a moment and with a large grin, his sky-blue eyes twinkled open, and he said, "From now on you will be known as Galaxy." That was certainly expansive. I liked the sound of Galaxy the Aquarian.

As we had filtered back from Maui, we had brought our new colored clothing with us—our whites destroyed by the rich, red Maui mud. With the shift to the music, Father felt it was time to shift color into our clothing, and we began experimenting with our styles being expressed in satins and silky fabrics in pastel colors.

Yahowha also saw it might be more attractive if he and his Suns dressed like the musicians of the day. Perhaps the public would be more receptive if we looked less like hippies. On the album *Kahoutek*, he sang, "Now there are those who will take it to the negative pole. They will remain in that hole they are in. But there are perhaps a few; As I look around, perhaps it's you; Oh God, I hope so; Oh God; I hope so." He knew—yes, perhaps hoped—there were to be more of us in the Family. So he commissioned a natural linen suit from a tailor for himself, while his Suns donned glam-rock-styled satin bell-bottoms and bright, flashy, silky shirts with platform boots. This change of clothes also posed a test to maintaining our consciousness and still being aware of our spiritual aims. Yahowha told us, "Never forget, you are in the world, not of it," as a reminder.

Eventually, he came up with the idea to play live gigs at local high schools and colleges. He thought it would be a great way to turn young people on to our brand of truth through our music. We held several free concerts on campuses around LA, events that attracted and dazzled the kids. The band played their spontaneous music, so we never knew what was in store. Yahowha's lyrics were often tailored to this younger audience, and when he started to play his kettle drum and the band followed along, it was mesmerizing for us. Many of the Family would tag along, and we stood out in the crowd because of our dress, filtering into the crowd to be available to them if anyone wanted to ask questions. Sometimes there was a flyer to hand out about our next show, but we always told them about the restaurant and our little store next to it to buy our albums. If someone was really interested, they might be invited to class.

Dawn Hurwitz

We pulled in a few more members with these activities, but for the most part, it was a hard truth we were living. Not everyone could get behind waking up at 3 a.m., taking a cold shower, exercising, meditating for a couple of hours, working in the restaurant, and then after only a few hours of sleep, starting all over again—24/7/365. The core members of the Family never had a problem with this; we were excited to wake up every day and spend our time with Yahowha and hear what came down for the day. The addition of music made us all the more excited to hear the teachings come down in song, often in metaphor. But even these new changes were not enough to keep some interested. They did not have to start out wearing white, and Yahowha said, "Those who come into the Family now do not need to walk the path the rest of us have before. They will fit right in." There was no mechanism in place that kept anyone captive. The only thing one had to do was be on our program. If not, they were invited to leave. Those who couldn't keep up with us often fled in the darkness of night.

At that point, Yahowha wanted the entire Family to have a classier update. Even though we were scrupulously clean, we were sometimes described as dirty hippies. He beckoned me into his room one day.

"Galaxy, I want you to buy three yards of velvet for each woman to make her own dress."

We listed every woman in the Family. Yahowha closed his eyes and visualized a color suited to their souls. Yahowha wanted to make a distinction, so velvet became our new fashion statement. It represented a richness in glorious colors, in contrast to our earthy homespun.

He divined me in gold. I did not love the dress I initially came up with. It morphed into a long skirt with a three-inch ruffled hem. I had much to learn about sewing velvet. It slipped around quite a bit and needed to be handled more precisely. The top had ruching along the shoulder seams with short sleeves and more ruching in the V neck. Designing often comes via a series of experiments. Some flowing gold satin better complimented the skirt. I constructed a bias-cut top with long fitted sleeves that crossed over itself in front, a peplum waist, and ruffles at the ends of the sleeve and around the neckline. It was my favorite, and I am so glad I have a photo of it because the outfit is long gone.

A family outing to Three Rivers, I'm wearing the rusty gold second from left of Yahowha.

A tiny store had been built adjacent to the restaurant to sell Family-made goods: records, jewelry, and clothes. I advertised my custom-made clothes there. At some point I worked there with Sunflower; not only was he the bass player in Yahowha 13, he was a jeweler and could construct almost anything. Sunflower had an acute, detail-oriented design ethic and made all of the Family's symbolic jewelry. Moreover, he built the Temple in the back of the restaurant above the storage shed, which was constructed entirely of redwood using no nails. Yahowha nicknamed him Golden Hands. He and I had a little "thing" that stemmed from my interest in learning from him plus our time together in Maui, but it never stuck.

Elliot Mintz came into our little shop wanting to have some velvet pants made for his job hosting the TV show "The Midnight Special." He knew Yahowha as Jim Baker from the days of the Old World Inn and the Aware Inn, Baker's former restaurants on the Sunset Strip. Elliot was a small man, boyish, very sure of himself, and very sweet. I did not know of his accomplishments.

He was a talent agent and deejay as well as a Hollywood reporter of all things modern, rock 'n' roll, and alternative. He represented John Lennon and Yoko Ono. We were just *so* into our own world that we

Dawn Hurwitz

Galaxy & Rain

never understood his importance! But I do remember the bell-bottom pants I made him. They were light aqua blue with rhinestones sprinkled down the sides. I was able to make a beautiful dress (pictured above) with the leftover materials. (I'm sure I bought too much fabric on purpose so I could.) It had a deep V neck, cold shoulders with long fitted sleeves ruched at the wrists, narrow lace trim around all the edges, and a splattering of the leftover clear, sparkling rhinestones scattered near the hem. It fit close on top but swept out to a wide swirl at the floor. I was only able to wear it once in a while as it became one of the more popular dresses in our now-shared closet.

Luckily other women in the Family sewed too—there were so many to clothe! I learned new skills from some and developed my craft. The most adept of us was Sunset. She had followed her two sons, Octavius and Sun, into the Family. In her forties, she was much older than most of us and was a Holocaust survivor.

At the close of World War II, she found herself in Paris working for an atelier. She knew how to make patterns, sew the tiniest seams, and produce luxurious styles from the most delicate fabrics. A photo of Aquariana, one of our Family's most angelic singers, shows her posing in a beautiful, robe-length, chiffon jacket on the cover of her album made from two layers of silk chiffon in pink and white with a long ruffle around the neckline. Silk chiffon is a very difficult fabric to sew. It pulls, has little stability, and the needle can leave large holes. It was Sunset's signature piece, and no one but Aquariana was allowed to wear it because it was deemed her "stage" cloak. Sunset was also tasked with making capes of caramel-colored alpaca or cashmere for the Council women, as it would cool down in the LA wintertime. She made five or six of them before plans were altered, and half of us never got them. We were supposed to share them, but they were mainly worn by the ones they were bestowed to.

Yahowha eventually wanted me to have my own line of clothing, which he named Crabtree Creations. It was an inside joke. His birthday was July 4, in the astrological sign of Cancer. He mused one morning that he felt like the hairy hermit crab who carried his home on his back, emerging with care and looking splendorous in the beautiful robes we had created for him. I designed a line of Grecian-inspired gowns made of a fabric called Quiana Jersey. It had a wonderful flow to it, was easy to care for, and was available in a myriad of colors. I designed one-shouldered dresses, caftans, and wraparound dresses that banded above the bust and left the shoulders free which could double as a skirt.

During one jam session, Yahowha came down with the idea to have a Council of twelve women, one for each zodiac sign. Makushla, his Mother Angel, would be the tiebreaker. The zodiac were his Wives and Mothers of the Family. His Suns' wives were Angels. Yahowha called them his Suns as their Angels revolved around them. It was a weird hierarchy that was a little awkward to get used to, and eventually, it created a rift that still exists today, which I have encountered as an "us/them" vibe with a few of the Angels. A core group of us conceived around the zodiac remained his Wives and Council members, but depending on the needs of different women, he tried to let them have an opportunity to be on the Council too.

It was all a part of the play, the great experiment. He wanted everyone to have equal opportunities, if possible. And he also felt that women should be able to choose whom they wished to be with. If a Sun wanted to be with a woman, he could flirt and hint at it, but ultimately it was always the woman's decision. The role of women in the Family was to serve the men. This included making and laundering their clothes, making their meals, massaging them at night, and being available for Sex Magic. In turn, the men were to provide and take care of the women, honoring them as the mothers of all living. The women who had children also took care of the children, and the women who did not worked in the restaurant waitressing.

When the women in the Family came to discuss problems with their relationships, Yahowha doled out advice. In that process, they became enamored of him, and his Suns often fell short because they could not leave their personality out of things and only show appreciation for their Angels. When anyone sat in front of Yahowha, they received his full, focused attention; thus, it was easy to feel his unconditional love. He did have a few crushes and often gave a woman an opportunity to be with him when he thought they wanted or needed to be. Sometimes they were in his inner circle for a week or so, sometimes only a day or two to experience what it was like.

This was becoming frequently unpopular with his Suns, who sometimes got confused and even a little angry. He would encourage the Council to be with his Suns, especially the ones who felt left out, as their Mothers. But all the women were running to Yahowha. It was hard for me to be with his Suns, and my relationships with them, while fluid, were affected by my feelings for him.

In my quest to be only with Yahowha, I would eventually sleep in the attic, library, and even on the meditation room floor by myself. I stored my bedroll. We did not have many personal items, perhaps as many as could fit in a cardboard box. Sometimes I stored a box above the cubbies and in the attic pushed under the curtain at the lowest pitch of the roof. We were encouraged to be non-materialistic: owning less brought you closer to God. I began to feel pent up and at loose ends. I tried to be with his Suns and attempted to give myself for short intervals to Sunflower, Djin, Rhythm, Gibraltar, Peace, and Octavius. Yahowha supported sexual freedom and believed there was no shame in finding affinities with anyone of the opposite sex in the Family, but our main relationship was with him. For me, it was hard to be in one with anyone else after being with the ultimate.

So the reason I was not in this now-infamous photo? It was just a day. Yahowha thought it would be an interesting juxtaposition to wear his new, custom-made suit for public situations, so he donned it, and the photo was taken on our patio for a Council portrait, which I was originally to be in.

At the last moment, he said, "Galaxy and Lovely, why don't you let Golden and Blessing (once Mutte) get in the picture?" They stepped in on the end at the left. He counted on me to not be overly sensitive or needy, that I would understand others needed to take their moment. So gracefully we stepped into the wings and watched it all happen. But on that day, it made me sad because it was always me who was the one to understand. I had to be strong, knowing his love for me did not waver, only my apparent position. These two women were only part of the Council for the rest of the day. They didn't last. But this picture will for eternity.

Dawn Hurwitz

20
Being with Yahowha

All I have to do is hear the first few bars of the song "Radar Love" by Golden Earring and these memories pour in. The Family thought it would be cool for Yahowha to have a white Rolls Royce. After all, the restaurant was making good money, and we felt it would be more fitting for him to ride around in style instead of his old VW bus. He asked Pythias to be his chauffeur and commissioned a cream-colored chauffeur's uniform with shiny brass buttons and a hat from his tailor. He saw Pythias as the driver of The Chariot Tarot card.

One day Yahowha asked Pythias to take me to get my driver's license. I was well past my seventeenth birthday and ready for it. In fact, Hypatia had patiently taken me out to teach me how to drive in one of the Family's cars. I had just completed a thirty-day water fast and felt svelte and really good about myself. I was mentally clear, strong, and now solidly one of Yahowha's women again. He knew I had little life experience beyond roaming the streets of Chicago and going to school and wanted this to be special for me. So there I was, rolling down the Sunset Strip in the back seat of the Rolls, with my first Family love, Pythias, at the wheel.

Pythias asked, "Would you mind if I turned the radio on?" He knew how much I loved music before joining the Family but did not want to assume.

I gleefully answered, "Turn it up!" Even though we did not listen to any music that originated from the Maya and existed outside our band room, I was up for it. Those notes beat out a moment eternally in my memory. I was driving with the man I came to LA to be with, and now I was with the Father of our Family, the teacher I had been seeking all along.

It could have felt weird, but it didn't. I felt a little strange at first, but I was comfortable with Pythias. He had Mutte and their new daughter, Ankha; I was with Yahowha. In those days it was so different. We were breaking the barriers of all the old social mores. Age did not matter, only chemistry. We were sincere—I was sincere. Later I found that not everyone was, but Yahowha was, as were most of the rest of us. We strove to create a new paradigm, which we attempted to build as Yahowha taught us to let go of our limitations. We had to experience situations that broke down what was considered normal in life to see if it expanded our ideals.

It is frustrating today when people ask, "Wouldn't you be furious if a fifty-three-year-old man was dating your sixteen-year-old daughter?" I suppose I might, but first of all, I do not have one, and second, it was my experience and felt right for me. These critics were not there; how could they know? They do not understand what it was like to break down the barriers of illusion, to not hold accountable the wheels of time, to only be in the moment and feel the truth and love in it. There was no harm in it. No one got hurt, and we all had a choice to be there. I am not going to play the Monday-morning quarterback and question my choices for that time.

In fact, I have just listened to a podcast story from *The Cults* on YouTube, episodes 77 and 78 on the Family, which included many facts about what the Family got into. But it placed such a negative spin on everything, claiming that Yahowha took advantage of us as if it was his master plan to dominate us. I know they took most of their information directly from Isis' book, as well as some of the more salacious elements from a disgruntled woman who had left the Family. They really built up the fact that Jim Baker had murdered two people. But what they neglected to say was that he had been defending women by using Jiu Jitsu—of which he was a master—and that he had been acquitted on both accounts.

I completely loved living in that time and in a communal life, where there was always someone around to help if I needed it. To trust and be trusted, to love and be loved, to have the cushion of a chosen family—all this soothed my soul. Someone always had my back, and we sincerely helped each other in our quest to live an idealistic lifestyle. Maybe it was the comfort I did not have in Chicago with my broken family, but it was mostly the spiritual aspect I was seeking. Historical scholars, like Timothy Miller in *The 60's Communes,* describe the Source Family and other groups like us not as cults but as "cultural reform movements" that proliferate in society during periods of societal breakdown and rapid change. There are so many negative things one could say about what happened back then, yet even more positive ones.

Yahowha used to say, "If you want to find something negative in a thing, surely you will find it. But it also corresponds that if you want to find something positive, there is so much more of that."

My mother had entrusted me to Father Yod because I had given up smoking cigarettes, smoking dope, doing drugs, and running amok on the streets of Chicago at all hours of the night. So many others in the Family have similar stories.

There are also the ones who have spent their entire lives unable to come to terms with the experience we shared. They choose to say bad things about everything that happened. Having been so influenced by those around them in the lives they embraced after the Family, they feel shame instead of joy at what they were able to learn from the experience. They make excuses for why they did it, saying they were under Father's spell. It is all about perception. If you look from the outside in and do not understand the story, it is easy to see it that way. I perceived it as the highest thing I could become a part of.

Yahowha held no one against their will. Everyone participated by their own choice. I do not see how anyone could say they were duped into it all and brainwashed. They were not. No one had to do anything they did not wish to. I remember once Yahowha wanted me to be with a Sun I had absolutely no chemistry with at all. I could not do it, and I told him so. Finally, he said, "You can't blame me for trying." He cared deeply for his Suns and was trying to share with them. He did not want the women all for himself.

I have been told this concept is coercive, weird, perverted, or worse. Not from my eyes. He reminded us over and over again, "This is all a big experiment. It hasn't been done before, so we have to create it. If it doesn't work, we can change it tomorrow." And we did. Unfortunately, not everyone was up for the experiment, so feelings got hurt, egos got twisted, and concepts were misinterpreted. But they should have known that he was open to everyone. Nothing was ever censured, except possibly to the public.

For instance, we did not talk about our sex practices publicly. We referred to it as Sacred Sex, ancient Tantric rituals designed to bring us together in physical, mental, and spiritual harmony. Today those rituals are being talked about so casually by people trying to see something horrendous in them. They were unusual but not horrendous. They were not satanic or done for selfish means; they were done to foster love, unite us, and help us survive as a family while learning and growing in our consciousness.

And then there were all the women. Yahowha had reached out to a couple of us; he had reached out to me. But I wanted to be there, I wanted him to reach out to me. All the women wanted to be with him, so it is understandable that his Suns felt deprived because the women all wanted to be with Yahowha and not them. He felt he could not turn the women down, and this was a problem until he conceived of the Council. That put a cap on it.

He treated each woman like she was the only one, every one of us. His focus was intense and brimming with unconditional love. He wanted his Suns to learn how to be this way. There were occasions when he saw a man and a woman he thought could be together. He would ask the woman if she would go and be with a certain Sun. Sometimes it worked out; sometimes it didn't.

Then came the Family caste system. It became kind of competitive—with the Suns, but also with some of the Wives and Angels too. The Aries position in the Council was bestowed on me (even though I am on the cusp of Taurus), but I still felt like I had to compete for my place with him. I felt his love for us was so big that we could all share it, but then I felt pushed aside by some of the women. Because I was so young, lacked self-confidence, and seemed frozen in some weird pecking order, I felt like the other women had more going on than I did. My Council sisters were mostly older, smarter, and more experienced.

I made Yahowha robes, gave him a sensual massage he could not resist, and combed his hair without making him wince. I was not as needy as some were, no longer needing to be constantly sitting at his side. And he loved my sensitivity; perhaps that was my value. After his first experiment with a second wife, I became the second woman to be with him alongside Ahom.

I asked him once, "Why do you let them all shove me to the back like that? Why don't you keep me closer?"

"You can't tell me that someone is actually shoving you out of the way?"

"Not exactly, but it feels that way. I'm always the last to be considered, to do things, or to be near you."

"They are all much less secure than you are. They need to feel closer."

But I still suspected that it was my lack of experience. I knew he loved me and kept me close, anyway, even when others wondered why I was with him.

This was an unprecedented modern-day situation only dealt with by Mormons and eccentrics. We were trying to build a new paradigm. It is hard for me to understand how anyone is ever really successful in multiple relationships. Communication alone takes up so much air.

21

Kauai

In the fall of 1974, Yahowha began talking about moving to Hawaii again, and it felt urgent. "I feel the coming changes and see the predictions of nuclear war beginning in the Middle East, combined with environmental changes due to the earth shifting on its axis. This will make Los Angeles an uncomfortable place to live." We were soon looking for another beachhead in Hawaii, and it turned out this time to be on Kauai.

Some suitable land was found and rented, thirteen acres with three houses and several outbuildings. He made the ultimate difficult decision to sell the restaurant and was on a plane with a small contingent a few days later at the end of December. The rest of us remained to work the restaurant until it sold.

Yahowha dreamed up a solid business plan. "We will build a geodesic dome community, using Buckminster Fuller's design. There will be several main domes to meet in, and we will have a restaurant and offer spa services to those who want to learn how to live a healthy lifestyle. We will teach them everything from eating raw, indigenous food to experiencing salt rubs, mud baths, and massage. There will be little auxiliary domes off the big ones where we can all live, and of course, we will grow all the food for the restaurant and ourselves."

He asked for a prospectus to be produced with artistic drawings of his vision along with a detailed business plan. We began sending out letters to people he knew who might be able to bankroll it. The only thing that happened was a buyer for the restaurant was located. Soon small groups of us were shifting over to Kapa'a, Kauai, our new home, as we could afford to send them. We left only a small crew at the restaurant during the transition. The new owners, The Pisces Corporation, bought the Source for $300,000, made a hefty downpayment, and would continue to send checks of $3000 every month until it was paid off. This allowed us to make the move and have a cushion while we were starting up.

I moved over a week or so after Yahowha did. I wish I could recall the circumstances but alas, I cannot. What I do remember is that again, we were in cramped conditions, but the air smelled sweet from all the green growing around us. The main house was not that big but had three bedrooms and a very large sunken living room, useful for meditation. A screened lanai sat on the end of it.

I asked where I was to sleep when I arrived and was told, "At night, you can find a space on the floor in the meditation room. You have to be up long before meditation though and have your bedroll and belongings put away. The small, third bedroom served as a sort of closet for the majority of us to stash our bedding and clothes. There aren't any other spaces available yet."

There were few spots on the floor or the screened lanai available, but I made do. Several of the so-called outbuildings were A-frame-type simple structures made of corrugated roofing and octagon-shaped wire mesh. We later found out they were originally intended to be chicken coups. Four people could occupy them as there were two long benches that could be used as a sleeping platform, and a bedroll could be laid on the ground for two. I slept on a bench one night and didn't need to do that again. It was hard, narrow, and felt too open to the elements.

The main house held Yahowha and Makushla in one bedroom and Ahom, Prism, and Aquariana with their babes in another. Ahom gave birth to the daughter she shared with Yahowha just before departing LA, and Prism and Aquariana were pregnant with Yahowha's babies and were due soon. One of the houses was designated for the other children and their mothers, who had been sent over first. Another house housed about sixteen people, sleeping toe to toe, as Electricity reminded me.

At least it was not like Maui, where all the floors were dirt except for those of the tents on platforms or the multi-leveled treehouse. We had electricity, running water, and a roof over our heads. For the first time, we were able to meditate every morning with Yahowha in Hawaii, and most of us were together. The men organized picking crews and would drive out searching for trees bearing fruit, bringing home avocados, papayas, and mangoes to feed the Family. They found some local families willing to share if we harvested their trees. Sometimes the extra produce was used to trade for other things like honey or coffee.

The last group to come over after the sale was completed packed up a couple of forty-foot shipping containers, placing two of the leased red-and-white VW vans in them along with the remainder of our belongings. The rest of our vehicles were put on the boat. I really do not know how we did it, but we made it happen. Where there is a will . . .

During the day we would walk the land. There was not much to do; we had no business and little transportation. You could take a hike down to the beach, but that was a couple of miles down the hill. At the entrance to our property, a wide lawn spread out with several large, old banyan trees. Their far-reaching branches gave some relief from the heat. We would walk up to a ridge on the property to watch the sunrise over the Sleeping Giant Mountain range, only the sleeping giant we saw had its hands held in prayer position over its heart, not the image most people see.

After our possessions arrived, Yahowha begged us to cull them even more, as we had nowhere to store them all. The pyramid that used to sit in the redwood temple behind the restaurant made with four of our triangular mirrors was to be one of the items deleted. Mercury came up with an idea. He and Thoth climbed the rugged mountain of the sleeping giant and placed it where its eye would have been. This became somewhat of a nuisance for some people when the sun reflected off of it, and no one could figure out what it was. No one tried to go up the mountain to find out. Mercury was able to do it because he had been a marine and nothing daunted him. Some years later we heard that a helicopter with a rifleman solved the problem, and the sparkle in its eye was no more.

The Suns found an old fishing boat for sale named the Shimni Maru. It came with a small airplane to spot the fish. Sunflower jumped at the chance to get his pilot's license, and the other Suns were happy to have some work to do that involved bringing home more food for the Family. Damascus donated the cash to purchase it, and the Suns found an old fisherman to teach them the ways of the sea. It turned out they were not very good at fishing.

We also tried to organize an island clean-up as a community service, asking the other hippie camps to join in and help pick up the garbage from the roadsides. That did not go down well with the hippies. They thought we were trying to recruit them—possibly a bit of truth, but not at a "you must join our Family to do this" level. It was to show the locals that we valued this sacred land by taking care of it.

But soon we started to feel threatened by some of the younger locals. Kauai is a small island, and word travels fast—they call it the coconut wireless. People would just appear in our driveway hoping to get a glimpse of all the beautiful, sexy, half- and sometimes completely naked women running around the compound. That was how we lived, doing our basic chores and taking care of the gardens, children, and our family needs. Being naked was sometimes practical as well as freeing.

Yahowha had the Suns place a round target at the bottom of the driveway by a tree to practice archery. One day Electra, one of the Family Angels, was walking down the road when a car stopped and a local flashed a gun in her face and told her she did not belong there. Yahowha decided to change the target to one in the shape of a human. The locals did not find that amusing, either.

We were chased off Kauai after these types of events, which culminated in a hundred-foot-long chain of lit firecrackers launched onto the roof of the children's house in the middle of the night. It sounded like machine gunfire. I awoke completely horrified. All of us were. They really did not like us, and Yahowha knew this would end badly if we did not leave. That moment was the turning point. The press had a heyday with us and reported negatively about us daily, which was not helping our credibility a bit.

Forty-two years later, I walked up the driveway to touch a tree on the thirteen acres that had finally ejected us from Hawaii, and it turned on the waterfall in my heart. I had never realized this had gone unprocessed. It had been kept damned up all those years, and at that moment, I had a shocking revelation that this had been the beginning of the end for the Source Family. I finally came to accept this.

Yahowha knew he had to find us a home somewhere else and thought that going to San Francisco, a large metropolitan area where we could blend in more easily, might be better. He flew over at the beginning of March 1975 with a small entourage. But one morning a few days after he had arrived, it came down that the only place he thought we would be safe was at the feet of the Himalayas, where alternative spirituality was accepted. He immediately made plans for visas, health certificates, and passports, with the first stop on his trek to Nepal being Tokyo. He left with an entourage to scout the new voyage, which he thought might take two months.

    I was left behind. Once again, I was not important enough to go with him and be by his side, but I was getting used to this by then. He taught us that space and time were an illusion. It is all a play, and we are just actors in it. So I played my part and waited patiently for the next act. After all, Nepal! That was exciting. One night after they had left, I walked up to the ridge during a full moon and saw Yahowha's face reflecting from the moon. He was there for me, and I just smiled knowing that.

22

Roots of Disillusionment

It started on Kauai, where, as a whole, we were completely rejected and displaced. Yahowha began to have doubts about who he was to us and the ultimate power he had. In his quest to be a God-Man, he became the word of God, which resulted in him discovering the pitfalls of ultimate power. For some innate reason, once Isis began treating him like Jesus, I never saw him as God incarnate. After that, I always felt he was a man with enlightenment holding pure intention and sharing what he saw.

In Kauai, all of these ideas came to an apex when he decided the answer was to flee and find us a new home. He got on a plane with an entourage of Makushla, Venus, Atla, and Tantalayo to San Francisco, meeting up with Damian and Damascus to join them en route to Nepal. Damascus had volunteered to finance the journey, still our financial angel.

In my quest to remember exactly what happened, I turned to the morning tapes, recently remastered by Karl Anderson. He had become a friend of the Source Family after working with Arelich (a.k.a. Sky Saxon, the front man for the band, The Seeds) on a music project. Isis felt he was the man for taking on the monumental task of several years of morning meditations or, as we commonly called them, class. She had several recordings for each day, some of them in better condition than others, and because they were not professional tapes, the sound quality was pretty bad. Karl spent thousands of hours bringing back the original sound without the static and editing out what did not need to be there, like long, silent pauses during our actual meditations.

Before Yahowha left Kauai, one of his Suns, Electron, a six-foot-six, hard-bodied ebony giant, took him aside privately and got into a confrontation with him. Yahowha retold it the next morning during meditation, and the following comes from these remastered tapes:

"You should have seen him, asking me for a thousand dollars, and he wouldn't tell anyone about what happened in the Family. I couldn't believe my ears. I didn't know what to do when I stood in front of him. Is that God? I am God and I am not God. I cannot lay my hand on Electron's head and say, 'Demon out!' Maybe I lack confidence?"

Electron answered, "I am just as much God as you."

"But if that's true, why can't we work together?" Yahowha replied.

"If I'm out of line, I want you to beat my spiritual ass," countered Electron.

"But I couldn't think of any way to do that. So I stayed in the silence," sighed Yahowha.

I believe this was the moment when his doubts surfaced. He had found that he had no real power; he could only speak his truth and seize opportunities to teach but had no real influence to effect supernatural change.

He said, "The Father of all knows best what you need and at the time you need it. Better even than I do. Man thinks I hold you together by some sort of mesmerism. It's love that holds us together. Without it would be chaos."

In a way, it was true. We were held together by the mesmerism of his love and wisdom and of his ability to speak with us honestly, no holds barred, even when he faced his doubts. He trusted us to go along on this wild ride with him, and we returned that trust.

I believe that was the moment we were put on the line to discover if love was truly what held us together. Without Yahowha there for us, we still meditated every morning, usually with one of the Suns leading the chants. With our dreams in flames, we were more on edge knowing that our days were numbered in Kauai and that we would have to be out of there soon or something bad would happen.

I have never examined this aspect of leaving Kauai before. Viewing it all now makes me see where I buried the grief and stuffed down the loss, too in shock from our hasty departure to deal with what had actually happened. This was where the song of the dream ceased. We had to flee our beloved islands, which were to be our refuge from the coming world tragedies—and which never transpired, of course. This was the moment we never could see at the time because we were all too wounded and had faith Yahowha was going to save us somehow.

Ahom called Yahowha in San Francisco before he departed in a desperate plea, asking him to send us a thousand dollars for food and basic supplies. We also heard that a welfare program often gave people money to go back to the mainland to get out of Hawaii. So, all of the mothers with children applied for welfare. When the authorities were contacted about the harassment we received from the locals, they practically laughed it off. Yahowha felt the island had put us in this situation of despair, so they could help us out of it. He also thought it was time for us all to be tested to see how we could handle it and would not send the money.

The men still organized picking crews to collect food across the island. Then the lease company who was leasing us our VW vans caught up with us and repossessed them because we had broken our lease agreement by taking them out of LA. We certainly couldn't afford to buy them! And so we were now down to one truck. Social services took care of the women with children, but that left a big gap for anyone without children. Some people called their parents, relatives, and old friends. We were still getting checks from the restaurant, but Yahowha had left using the last one. The Council had to wait for the next one to appear. Then we had to get air reservations, which involved going from Kauai to Honolulu to San Francisco, where we would meet up with Yahowha after his round-the-world journey.

A few of us who got out of there early found some apartments in Corte Madera for us to land. The building was about fourteen stories and faced a major roadway, but it was something. The apartments filled up as contingent after contingent landed there.

In the end, we escaped our dream and flew to San Francisco, ending up compressed into four apartments just off the Golden Gate Bridge. More than one hundred people, plus children and babies, were crammed into every possible nook and cranny like sardines. I recall sitting on the floor with my back against a couch and just enough room to cross my legs beneath me. Won, our Family humorist, and performer, was so small that he squeezed himself up on top of the refrigerator. It was temporary, and it was uncomfortable. Hawaii was over, and we were all bummed.

Yahowha returned at the end of April and told us all about his grand expedition, which had left San Francisco on March 7, 1975. He did meet Ahom briefly at the Honolulu airport layover, probably to give her some cash. The party had then jetted off to Tokyo and meandered to Hong Kong, Bangkok, New Delhi, Katmandu, and Pokhara, Nepal, spending only a day or two in each place.

Things were not as he had hoped. The cities were dirty and full of disease. He was seen as a God-man at every port of call and received the respect he thought he was due. But that was not enough. These places were all third world, and Yahowha did not want this for his Family, who were used to living a richer, safer, lifestyle. When they returned to India and visited Calcutta, Darjeeling, New Delhi, and Bombay, Yahowha began to feel the weight of his entourage, like too much baggage. Perhaps he felt too distracted by them and wanted to get a clearer view of what to do next, so he sent Venus, Tantalayo, and Atla back to Kauai. Damascus had already returned to LA earlier for business.

Yahowha continued on with only Makushla and Damian, eventually landing in Cairo on Easter Sunday. Makushla saw to his needs, and Damian took care of arrangements, leaving him free to ponder. However, when they landed in Cairo with no reservations, they discovered the hotel was fully booked, so their cab driver offered that they stay with him.

They wasted no time and asked to be taken to the pyramids, arriving just after sunrise. No one else was in sight. A man who seemed as if he had been waiting for them appeared from a doorway of the pyramid and said, "Follow me." He led them on a private tour deep into the unknown chambers of the pyramid. The deeper they tread, the more they all fell into a heavily altered state, like some sort of spiritual initiation, culminating in feeling as if they were the Father, Son, and Holy Ghost. When the guide led them through a side door to the exit, Yahowha turned to thank the man, who told him, "Yes, you are Jesus."

After their twenty-four hours in Cairo, they continued their journey through mainland Europe, England, Canada, and then onto the Pacific Northwest before landing back in San Francisco. Yahowha said he could find no place that felt right for his Family to be safe as we all gathered to hail his return at the San Francisco Airport.

They arrived home with their luggage filled with all sorts of treasures. While in India, Yahowha had wanted the women in his entourage to dress like the Indian women, and they shopped for saris. Makushla made sure to bring back a bunch for the Council to share. We were all fascinated with how to wear them; mostly made of silk chiffon, they were very slippery and needed to be folded and tied precisely or they would slip apart. So beautiful in deep colors of pink, turquoise, emerald, and indigo, our saris had gold and silver beading, sequins, and embroideries. We wore them with leotards because it was too cold for the midriff-baring tops. In Nepal, the entourage had discovered long, woolen coats with beautiful embroideries around the collars and cuffs, and down the front. Because San Francisco was a bit cooler, they held onto those, while the rest of us shivered.

Yahowha in class at a Mill Valley home

Yahowha's return to San Francisco six weeks after he had left was a huge relief for us all. But now we had to vacate the Corte Madera apartments, where we had worn out our welcome again: there were too many of us. We spent a couple of nights in Astral's parents' home in Mill Valley while they were away, but the neighbors called the cops, and we had to leave. Yahowha decided to call upon the mercy and hospitality of the area churches in Marin County. We spent our nights in one church and then another, sleeping in pews, aisles, and wherever else there was a space. We called this journey "forty days and nights in the desert" (in reality it was only about two or three weeks), and we likened ourselves to the wandering Jews. But I was just happy that Yahowha was with us now and we were sharing this together.

Sitting at the feet of Yahowha in a treasured sari after a morning meditation in a church

A large panel truck was rented to contain all our baggage, and we tried to keep everyone fed with a roof over their heads at night. In fact, one of the women ended up giving birth in one of the churches, as we only practiced home birth. She was at least surrounded by the love of our Family. To say it was uncomfortable is an understatement.

This was San Francisco, though, and most people there were used to hippies and eccentrics. Many of the residents of Marin were themselves. The churches humored us, offering an overnight charitable stay, and the communities in which the churches were located found us interesting and came out to talk with us as we milled around the grounds.

One could easily get whiplash, bouncing from one reality to the next. Even though it may have seemed cruel or ridiculous, Yahowha had a plan, even when he did not immediately let on to it or possibly realize it himself. He wanted us to truly learn to live in the moment. To do that, we had to never look back, stand firm where we were, and take ultimate responsibility for the moment. He would say, "What is responsibility but the ability to respond? How do you respond, with emotion and a knee-jerk reaction? Or do you look for the logical steps to take in the situation?" We landed at the Atherton Mansion standing tall, looking around us to see what needed to be handled in the moment.

The Atherton Mansion today.

23

The Atherton Mansion

The large, old house was located on the corner of California and Octavia Streets in the city. It was said a ghost roamed the halls—and especially the "witch's hat" turret on the corner of the manse. Legend has it that old man Atherton's son had been returned from a voyage at sea in a barrel of rum to preserve his body and was delivered to the front landing.

The original estate had forty-nine acres surrounding it. Little by little, the owners had probably sold it off to the city until all that was left was the house that occupied the corner of those streets. It was a humungous house and had been divided up into thirteen apartments. Plus, it contained a large basement.

Finally, we had a little breathing room again. The band set up in the basement, and we were able to stretch out and regroup. The entry hall was gigantic, with beautiful wood trim everywhere and a big fireplace, and we could all meet there and have meditation in the mornings. A block up the hill was Lafayette Park, where we could go out, get some fresh air, and take the children out to be in nature. This was something new for me. I had not experienced this in San Francisco on my journey to the Family in 1972.

The Family felt safe here. We could start again. Our journey had tested some who had not been with us for that long, and they fled. But a hardcore group of a little over a hundred of us, who had lived through the Mother House, and the Father House, and the Maui trek, and our final test on Kauai, still stood together in that spring of 1975. When I first walked up to the mansion right on the main street in the middle of town, it spoke of an older era of the city. A solid brick wall surrounded the corner. Its large ornate architecture and girth made me stand back in wonder. There were so many windows and articulated levels of rooms instead of a flat-fronted building. Little gingerbread details could be found under the rooflines and in the carved ornamental trim. A set of double-wide, cement stairs led up to the doorstep of the house, which was built into a hill. The large double doors were welcoming, making me feel like there was going to be room for us all—no more stacking up on top of each other like sardines.

Yahowha, Pythias, Sunflower, and Octavius in the basement of the Atherton Mansion

The first step was to make sure everyone had a suitable place to be. As there were thirty-five rooms, that was not a problem. An elegant wooden staircase wound up to the second floor from the entry hall, and an open hallway gave entrance to the second-floor rooms. Yahowha took the bedroom just below the witch's hat turret and had the inside of the turret painted black to meditate in. We put up a wallpaper of flocked velvet on burnished gold above the wainscoting in his bedroom.

The mansion was sadly in a deteriorating state, which may have been why we were able to rent it for only a thousand dollars. In fact, we also had the option to buy it. The Suns were more than up to the task of rejuvenating it and received several jobs from locals who noticed how hardworking they were. Herb Kane lauded us in his news column, noting how the city appreciated that we had saved the house from the wrecking ball and real-estate developers.

The once ballroom off of the wide-swept entry hall had been an apartment for an older woman with an untold number of cats who were not well-tended. The stench in there was atrocious! Isis had been allergic to cats and decided that the only way for her to get over her allergies was to occupy the space and let her body build up immunity to it. I thought she was very brave. Although I was not allergic to anything, the smell of that room put me off entirely. Osiris helped her clean and paint it to a point of bearability, and a few other folks eventually moved in there too.

Hypatia and I opted for the room on the opposite end of the landing from Yahowha's, which had been reserved for the nursing mothers of his children and had enough room for a few of his women. I could live there, listening to the sounds of babies who were not always content, or I could move in with Isis, which was not even an option for several reasons. Beyond the cat odor, I did not want to be under her eye, constantly ready to be busted for any little infraction of the rules. After all, she still had her radical belief that Yahowha was God incarnate. So I ended up spending as much time as I could up the hill at Lafayette Park, just blissing out under the intoxicating aroma of a Wisteria bush. It took me away to a happy place almost like a drug.

The children were all organized to live in another of the big suites, and a classroom was designated in the basement. Couples spread out in all the rooms. Along with the new band room, there were a few more spaces in the basement that some of the single men opted for. Unlike Maui, Kauai, and the Father House, we finally had a little more room to spread out. It was even bigger than the Mother House. We had just been through shock treatment and needed some time to recoup and plan our next future, now that all the other plans had failed us.

Yahowha would sit in front of the giant wooden fireplace in the entry room and hold Morning Meditation. The floor was tiled and a little hard to sit on, but a blanket and pillow helped that. We were all down to bare bones at this point though, after having sold everything except what could fit into one cardboard box per person in Kauai. But we were together, and Yahowha had returned. We couldn't wait to hear the next plan come down.

In the audience at Golden Gate Park. In front, L-R
Rythm, Rain, Galaxy, Yahowha

We took long walks in the city, up and down nearby Union Street and sometimes all the way to Fisherman's Wharf. The Suns kept trying to get jobs and even went to thrift stores to get clothing to easily blend in as regular hippies. They had sparse resumes with only restaurant experience—useful only for work at a fast-food place, which was against all our principles. Joshua came up with the idea of importing honey from Hawaii and selling it to stores and even out of backpacks on the street. But jobs eluded them, and our cash reserve was dwindling fast.

Yahowha became disturbed that his Suns were not getting it together as he would have. He had less interest in singing with the band and only recorded one more record with them, *The Operetta*. Meanwhile, the musicians were inspired. Lovely had finally returned after turning eighteen, free now of her father, Andre Previn's, reins. She brought her violin, formed a band named Breathe with Hom, and began playing gigs. They even played a gig at Golden Gate Park. Still, it did not pay much.

24

On the Road Again

I got used to San Francisco and found ways to handle the Hawaii disconnect. I happily volunteered to run errands to pick up anything we needed. It gave me an excuse to go out wandering. Window shopping on Union Street was fun and a good getaway. Lafayette Park and its insistent aroma of Wisteria was my other. Everyone knew where I might be if I wasn't around—not that anyone ever went looking for me. I think everyone was looking out for their own concerns, and Yahowha had plenty of other women to care for him. In fact, I grew weary of the constant jostling to be near him. Much as I hoped to have children myself, I had to get away from those babies, who needed so much attention, and their mothers, who were all too quick to hand them over to anyone who was nearby. So I found it best to stay out of the way. A small part of me was jealous; they had his babies, and try as we did, I was barren.

It was more difficult getting used to the constant chill in the air and having to wear a couple of layers to be comfortable. I have craved being in the sunshine since I was small, and Hawaii spoiled me. Even when it rained, it was warm. At least I could wear the long dresses and velvets that were too warm to wear in Hawaii.

△ ▽ △ ▽

My dad surprised me with a visit from Chicago. He was in town for a business meeting and wanted to spend the day.

"Have you been for a drive down Lombard Street yet?" he asked.

"No. We only have one van that's always used to pick up supplies or other things. I only go where I can walk," I lamented.

He said, "Why don't I pick you up? I have a rental car, and we can take a drive down there. I also want to see Coit Tower, and we could go have lunch."

"That sounds good. I never get a chance to eat in a restaurant, anymore. Can I bring Hypatia along? She and I are close, and she could use getting out too. You'll like her! She's a lot of fun."

I enjoyed spending time with him. He had finally given up on any ideas that I might leave the Source, so we had an easy exchange all day—and it was interesting to see some more of San Francisco. A photo reminds me of the day. Hypatia and I had a good time escaping the confinement of the Family for a moment.

It was not that the Family was hard to be around. We still got up and meditated with Yahowha every morning. It was just that the tension began building as we wondered what we were going to do at our new location. I certainly felt at loose ends. With no money for fabric to make clothes, I was constantly seeking distraction aside from the duties I performed in the house, which were either laundry or babysitting.

Galaxy & Hypatia

Nothing was panning out for the men as far as jobs went. Yahowha was frustrated by their lack of success.

He brainstormed how the new band, Breath, would land a contract and make money with their music—till that didn't materialize. Then he talked about having someone buy out the contract for the rest of the money owed from the sale of the Source Restaurant. When that looked like it would happen, he began thinking about Hawaii again, only a little differently.

"We will buy houses. That's the way to go. There's a house we can put a downpayment on, and also, the ones on either side of it are available. The Big Island will be different. We can buy several houses, so we won't have to live so cramped together anymore and can live separately." he said.

We heard from our "spiritual cousins," the Love Family in Seattle, that the Big Island was a good place to be and we could move into the house they were vacating across from the ocean. We called it the Sake House. It had been known as the Tea House, but somehow it got mistranslated. Yahowha, Makushla, Isis, and a few other women went over first at the end of June 1975. I followed with the rest of his women several days later.

The home was a capacious four bedrooms, a great-room living area, and a small garden. Best of all, we could get in the ocean every day across the street. It was a good landing spot and had plenty enough room for the Council, but we needed to find something appropriate, something that would fit the entire Family.

Electricity came over and developed a relationship with a realtor, Dwayne Carlsmith, who had recently bought a house called the Doc Hill Mansion down the street from us right on the ocean. He allowed us to rent it temporarily to give us a start, as he was not ready to move in. It had a tremendous entry hall that must have been forty feet long by twenty-five feet wide—perfect for morning meditation—with a tall, wooden, peaked ceiling and lava rock walls. Multiple glass doors opened to a lawn overlooking the ocean. It was perfect. The kitchen was designed for a professional chef, with lots of storage and counter space. There were several bedrooms on one end and several more on the other, a roomy garage, and a hulking greenhouse on the side—plenty of room to transform into living spaces. The Family commenced making plans to get to Hilo, with Yahowha asking everyone to be there by August 1, and we moved in immediately.

The backyard was a small grassy patch upon a great lava rock wall butting right into the ocean with steps leading down for access. But I soon found that diving in when the tide got high was much more fun. We were situated on a small bay where the manta rays liked to swim in and out. Being at close range with the ocean was the best part of that house.

Everywhere we had gone, Yahowha had always admonished, "Leave this place in better condition than we found it." This was true

Psychedelic Wild Child

in Los Angeles when we left the Mother House and Father House. And even though we were chased off Kauai, we cleaned the buildings there well. In fact, the Atherton Mansion was deemed no longer destined for demolition after our upgrades and still stands proudly today like the grand old dame she was. At our core, we maintained a strong workforce because Yahowha instilled a healthy work ethic in us all, and in Hilo, again, it caught our neighbors' eyes. The Suns began a work crew and were offered jobs. Joshua was inspired to start a bakery named Goodies with an investment from a local businessman who was impressed by us. A storefront was found, and we began distributing our bread to the local health food stores. Our bakery became known for organic whole-wheat bread, rolls, and healthy pastries.

Yahowha and the Council at Doc Hill Mansion: Isis, Paralda, Harvest Moon, Ahom & Tau, Prism & Buttercup, Tantalayo, Astral, Yahowha, Makushla, Aquariana & Yod, Galaxy, Venus, Lovely, Hypatia, Heaven

Yahowha continued to be restless. I don't know what happened to the house that we were going to buy, but like everything else, we moved on quickly. "Change is the order of the universe," was Yahowha's battle cry.

Mercury had met a man on Oahu who was into hang gliding, and he became fixated on the sport. He started flying with the man off of the small hills surrounding Kailua and finally off the cliffs of Makapu'u, which are 1300 feet up from the beach. Yahowha told us that we were once the Lemurians, an ancient culture in the Pacific that predated Atlantis and had the ability to fly. Anxious to watch Mercury in action, Yahowha flew to Oahu with Makushla, Isis, Venus, and Electra to observe Mercury while he broke the world record for hours aloft.

Once more, I was not included to go. I was one of the younger ones and did not have the life experience, which paradoxically would have qualified me to get some experience. But by this point, I accepted my second-tier consideration and expected it.

Mercury was staying with his new friend who had rented a beautiful home in Lanikai, and when Yahowha and company arrived, they were invited to stay there too. Its modern, round structure had a cone-shaped roof, and it perched like a nest atop a hillside overlooking the sparkling, turquoise bay. Lanikai translates to "heavenly waters," which they were. Originally a small weekend getaway enclave on the windward side of Oahu, it had now become a bedroom community. Yahowha spent his days taking walks down the hill to the fine sand beach for long strolls and swimming in the gentle ocean. There was no negative attention from the residents. Yahowha fell in love.

Mercury's friend fell in love with Yahowha, who named him Jupiter. I believe the beautiful women in his entourage also helped—Jupiter was quite the ladies' man—and so began our migration to Oahu. He brought the rest of the Council over in the course of a week. Even though he had asked the entire Family to be in Hilo by August 1, 1975, he was in Lanikai with the entire Council and a new plan by then.

25
The Startling Truth

After combing the world for a place we could call home, live comfortably together, and have a business to live our ideals, we ended up in Lanikai on Oahu. It was across the Pali from Honolulu on the windward side past Kailua, a tiny gem of an ocean community. One road winds into it along the foothill and loops around at the end to return out on the side where the homes' backyards are the glittering bay. Surrounded by thousand-foot hills, the small valley floor was a sleepy beach town in those days, with a shoreline occupied by houses mostly meant for large families to gather for weekend retreats. The gentle waves broke on the finest, baby-powder-like sand.

About a mile out, a reef protected the bay from the big waves. At the reef's edge stood two small islands called the Mokaluas. They appeared in silhouette as a pyramid and sphinx.

Jupiter's rental, the Round House, sat on the hill rising up the mauka (mountain) side. He had been a stuntman in Hollywood and made good money to afford this idyllic hideaway. The house bore a sweeping view of the ocean and the entire community. Its front was arced with floor-to-ceiling windows around the large, open living/dining/kitchen area, with a wide surrounding deck outside. Jupiter was often away working, and there was plenty of room for Yahowha and his women. Morning meditations were so magical in that spot, where we could watch the sun rise up out of the sea from the lanai.

I was delighted to feel, at last, a solid part of his circle. With only three bedrooms in the house, Yahowha slept in one and nursing mothers in the second, with storage in the third. The rest of us sprawled on the living room floor. Jupiter was a little miffed at losing his bedroom, but he soon got over it as he fell deeper in love with Yahowha and the enchantment of all the women around him.

I was so happy to be with Yahowha and his women. It was just us—even though it was a big us! Duties were assigned, and I ended up with laundry, as usual, but I liked that I was able to get out and see what was going on in our closest little town of Kailua.

It was a utopia for a few short weeks. After our chores were complete, we spent our days strolling down the soft sand to where it ended in rocks and the little Flat Island came into view that sat about fifty yards out in the bay at the gateway of Lanikai at the end of Kailua. We then cooled off in the calm waters and returned. When Yahowha walked up and down the beach with his contingent of women and babies in tow, it certainly brought out the curiosity of the community. Lanikai was the kind of place where everyone smiled, waved, and said good morning. We met many people that way, and mostly they accepted us, at least superficially. Some did not, but they seemed harmless, just going about their own business and ignoring us. Many knew Jupiter from his time living there already. Tall and handsome with a chiseled face, long, shaggy, sun-bleached hair, and sweet, understanding eyes, he had already attracted his own attention.

As we walked down the sand one day, Yahowha looked at me and said, "You can eat anything you'd like if you swim to Flat Island every day." I was tired of shuffling from one diet to the next just because I was built a little bit bigger than many of his women. Plus, I loved being in the water, where I felt free and one with nature. He knew that.

Jupiter had a friend named Vern who lived in a beach house down the hill from us and always welcomed us, speaking of Yahowha with envy. He was also a handsome guy and in his mid-forties, much closer to Yahowha in age. His looks and demeanor reminded me of the movie star James Coburn. Yahowha invited him to class one morning, where he accepted Yahowha as his spiritual Father and was promptly named Cygnus. He could not make it to class every morning and so became a bit of an outsider, but he was always so hospitable to us that Yahowha kept him as an ally in the community.

It was the height of the heat in August 1975, and Yahowha had felt stifled for days. During morning meditation, he would go within and find nothing new to share, so we often sat in silence, awaiting his latest missives that never came. Maybe he was missing the rest of the Family. He would cheer up when new people were invited and would recount all his basic teachings and ask them about their lives.

Our August 25 morning meditation was especially quiet. We took our six-second hit of the sacred herb, chanted, and went into meditation, waiting for Yahowha to channel the wisdom of the moment soon thereafter. Yet again, nothing came.

Makushla, Yahowha, Ahom, Galaxy.

He startled us and spoke up with urgency. "I have nothing left to teach you. I've given you all I have received. It's time for you all to leave the nest." We did not take that too personally, as he often spoke with the intent that it would be heard by the rest of the Family on tape. "Makushla, you have dressed appropriately for today." (She had worn black). "Mercury, let's go." When Yahowha was on the move, everyone moved quickly to keep up with him. With his strapping, six-foot-four height, and a sure and athletic gait, it had to be amusing to watch us all mobilize around him. There were his thirteen Wives, three babies, and Mercury. (Jupiter was away.) Hastily picking up whatever we may have needed for this spur-of-the-moment, unknown journey, we all piled into the Mercedes, a van, and another car. The van had a kite strapped onto its roof rack.

We sped into the breaking daylight to Makapu'u cliffs along the ocean and then up the long winding road behind it to the summit. Arriving at a locked gate at the top, we entered when another glider with keys let us drive through. The sun began to rise as we got to the top of the cliff. The coast looked magnificent as the sun quickly rose from the sea. Yahowha had accompanied his Suns many times on their flights, and unbeknownst to the rest of us, he had planned one for himself, with only Mercury in his confidence.

Mercury busied himself with setting up the kite while all of us women questioned Yahowha as to why he thought he could do this. An uncertain tension permeated us. Mercury was struggling to keep the kite anchored while the wind whipped up aggressively. He hung on Yahowha's every word and direction and acted on them. This was all so surreal. I couldn't really grasp what was happening as I struggled to remain in the moment. What were we to do? All of us women pleaded with him to not do this. He took no notice and kept saying that all would be fine and was as it should be. We would all be taken care of as we always were. There was no stopping him. The thirteen of us women were surrounding Yahowha, with Makushla leading the battle cry, "No, Yahowha, you're not really going to do this" to no avail. The kite was ready, Yahowha was primed, and the wind swiftly lifted the kite in the air as we watched, astounded, as Yahowha rose away from the cliff.

Atop Makapu'u Cliff awaiting the inevitable.
Me looking up in the center

26

Suspended Animation

Time stood still as everything advanced in slow motion. Yahowha ascended like a butterfly, catching the wind and rising away from the cliff. I can't imagine the exhilaration he must have felt at that moment. Was it worth it to take such a risk? We all found little perches to watch him from on the edge of that cliff, shielding our eyes from the morning sun that was rising. He was just hovering over the hillside. And then we became aghast as the wild wind came to an abrupt halt. The thirteen of us stood frozen as one body, taking note of every detail of what followed in complete, awestruck silence. Helplessness shuddered through us as we watched Yahowha struggle with the kite, trying to steer its nose up in his rapid descent. He seemed about fifty feet above the ocean when the nose finally lifted, but not without the frame being bent in the process, as we discovered later. He soared up and out across the ocean, then swerved the kite around toward the shore, leaving a flight path in the shape of a question mark. He then skidded down onto the beach parking lot, and in one movement, we got into the vehicles and took off racing down the hill, which seemed to take forever. We parked the cars haphazardly and raced to the lot near his landing spot, where the Hawaiians and Samoans camped for the summer.

We discovered him alone, lying on the grass of the beach park, the locals surrounding him in a wide circle. No one went to his aid. They parted as we spilled from our vehicles, running to his side. He asked us not to block the sun so he could feel it on his face. We asked if he was all right, where it hurt, was he able to move. He answered in a wispy tone, "Where did that angel go who helped me down?" There was no one, just the wide-eyed locals standing back and staring in disbelief at this huge man dressed in maroon and black velvet robes who had fallen from the sky into their camp. A jolt buzzed through me; I felt useless and once again pushed aside by the rest of the women angling to get near him. He was asked if he wanted to go to the hospital, and he replied tersely, "Take me home."

We banded together, and now they needed me—or my strength—as we grasped arms, legs, and torso, carefully carrying him to the Mercedes just as the fire department and ambulance arrived. We practiced natural healing with no chemicals and wanted to escape any kind of situation with the authorities, and narrowly escaped, assuring them that he was okay and we were taking him home.

Our arrival at the Round House was mayhem. Awkwardly we carried his large frame up the steep wooden steps to the house, squeezing him as we all struggled to carry him up. All of us ladies were clad in nightgowns, the wind whipping around us as we grasped the man whose immense body was in pain and unwieldy. A quilt was spread on the living room floor, and we laid him down on it as gently as possible, as he directed. Then he closed his eyes and entered into a deep trance.

We were unsure what to do next. Someone flashed that he might want some oxygen, and when he perked up to say yes, we called an ambulance to bring some. By some miracle, they did not interfere to take him away. I'm sure they had never encountered a situation like this before; it must have been enough just to witness. Thirteen beautiful women in flimsy nightgowns, with obviously nothing on underneath them, directed the activity like a hive of bees around a man that looked like God lying on the floor, and only one other man there, Mercury, acting as the fiercest sentry ever. We stuck to our belief in managing things as naturally as possible.

Yahowha couldn't get comfortable. Every little move he made pained him, and he wanted to get out of his clothes. We carefully lifted his robes up over his body as he leaned with great effort from one side to the other in order to maneuver the robe off. He asked for a shawl and just wanted to lie there like that, and said, "There is a great energy circulating at the base of my spine."

Makushla sat by his side with a goblet, offering sips of water, asking what he wished for next.

"I need you all to sit back and give me some air."

Isis thought to call Yogi Bhaghan, Yahowha's spiritual father, who said, "Give him some cell salts and teas", and someone was dispatched to obtain them. Stanley Burroughs, a well-known natural healer who lived in the area and was famous for his lemon, maple syrup, and cayenne health drinks, was summoned and brought his light-therapy machines. The women took careful effort to get Yahowha comfortable, shifting him so Burroughs could focus the light at the base of Yahowha's spine, where he had the most pain. After some time, Burroughs realized this was out of his element. There was nothing more he could do, and so he gracefully left, wishing us well.

The buzz between the women was like a live wire. The nursing mothers were the most on edge, while the rest of us felt the urge just to be there and observe, ready to do anything that needed to be done. This process went on for almost eight hours. In the end, Yahowha mumbled a private, inner conversation with an unseen soul and chanted, "It is not my will, Father, but thine," repeating this over and over again. Finally, he went silent, and still, and his last breath exhaled. His spirit left his body and us.

Unfortunately, I did not get to experience that moment. As the afternoon wore on, the nursing mothers were so wound up in their agitation that they demanded that Paralda and I run out and do the laundry because they needed clean diapers. Neither of us wanted to go, yet under pressure we relented. We did not want to miss anything but rationalized that Yahowha would just pass through all of this and survive. On our return, we walked through the door with bundles of clean laundry to witness several women trying to maneuver Yahowha's body to give him an enema. He had always told us that this should be the first thing to do when a body dies to slow down the decomposition in the intestines, as it was to be chanted over for the following three days.

What a sobering moment! Those bundles of laundry just hit the floor. I do not remember focusing on anything but the process in front of me. I had done my duty: if the mothers wanted their clean diapers, there they were.

Yahowha was free of this world. I felt oddly relieved and ultimately left out of the final experience of his soul leaving his body. He was finally able to let go and move on from his pain and the frustrations of the Family's lack of success. He often talked of building a new home on Sirius for us in the next life. I truly believed he would. Looking back, life is so tenuous, and no one knows what will happen. It is all a possibility; we can believe whatever we wish to believe. But now I am prepared and have no expectations. Death is the final big adventure.

Yahowha prepared us well for this possibility. He often taught on the subject of death and how it should be handled. We knew what to do. We had to remain calm, in our centers, and act responsibly, observing but not reacting.

At first, it was just the Council of Thirteen Wives and a shattered but stalwart Mercury. We needed a few more Suns to help us. A phone call was made to the Doc Hill mansion, and Damian picked up. He was already feeling something was up and poised to take action. Other Family members gathered around to listen as he relayed the news. A wave of utter disbelief blew over them initially, thinking it was a bad joke. Damascus, Pythias, and a few others immediately flew over from the Big Island to help with the cremation arrangements and logistics.

Meanwhile, we cleaned his body and prepared a final ritual to release his soul, allowing Yahowha's body three days to rest and review his river of life, complete his journey on earth, and allow his soul to ascend in peace. We placed him on his bed, and chanted over his dead body, placing candles at his head and feet and surrounding him with an abundance of fresh, fragrant flowers. To this day the smell of tuberoses brings me directly back to that moment.

Over the next few days, I observed his skin turn more translucent and paler as the light of his being faded. His body was now a shell, and his soul was in transition. We all took turns chanting an hour at a time. He taught us that death was like moving from one room into another. Suddenly it was all so very real. I had no idea what was to come, much less the ability to imagine it.

An abrupt change was about to take place. He had taught us that

The Council's last picture together. From back L: Aquariana, Yod, Paralda, Tanatalayo, Makushla, Astral, Isis, Heaven, and Lovely. Front: Harvest, Hypatia, Tau, Buttercup, Ahom, Prism, Galaxy

change is the order of the Universe, and we had gained the security of knowing that we would just handle it by living in the moment. I finally shed a few tears, in the stark realization that he would no longer be there for me. He had always known my love and devotion and had been my champion. But I had felt like the lowest one on the totem pole of the thirteen, as one of his younger wives. Now I would have to fend off the Council and the rest of the Family to maintain my status. Often, they had not understood me; Yahowha was my focus and the reason I was there. So I would have to refocus and learn to be more open to the whole.

But what on earth were we going to do next?

When the three days were over, an ambulance was called to pick up his body for cremation. Instantly, the news went public. The media were calling, and the coconut wireless set the community on alarm. An article announcing his death appeared on the front page of the Honolulu Advertiser that gave blow-by-blow accounts of our actions. They were kind enough to tell without judgment how we had handled his death and claimed no wrongdoing on our part, only that an autopsy would determine if there were any criminal charges. As the law stood, it was a crime not to report a death after twenty-four hours. And right next to the article was this headline: "New Star Shines Its Light on Hawaii." It seems that the star, also described as a nova, had appeared in the constellation Cygnus and was as bright as the major stars. This was a sign to us that he had successfully moved on, and it was an additional omen for me.

As no foul play could be found by the authorities and no broken bones were discovered in the autopsy report, no one could determine what killed Yahowha. The entire island of Oahu had been talking about us, but soon they seemed to get over it, and everything settled down after a week or so. We had had our "fifteen minutes," becoming the offbeat neighbors in the Lanikai landscape for a while. People would stare and whisper to each other. We would smile back at them, and they would have to smile back.

Then the eviction notice arrived to vacate the Round House. We had nowhere to go and barely enough time to grieve and regroup. Plus, we didn't have enough cash to rent another house, not to mention the fact that no one would rent to us when they found out who we were. So Cygnus generously offered for us to stay down at his house for a few weeks while we figured out our next action plan.

Meanwhile, back in Hilo, Dwayne Carlsmith was ready to move into the mansion with his Family but found us a new place to live, the old Hilo Country Club a few miles above Hilo town for only $35 a month!

The Council & Mercury watching the ambulence leave.

27

Wandering

Staying at Cygnus' house was a refreshment we all desperately needed. It healed us to be right at the water's edge, swimming, doing sand scrubs, and walking along the shoreline, cleansing ourselves of trauma. We talked about what to do next. It was hard to see where we were going and what Yahowha would want us to do. We felt he would want us to continue his mission of finding a place where we could all live together and thrive in the teachings and keys of life he had bestowed on us. But some had different ideas and there were always financial restraints.

After a couple of weeks, Cygnus informed us his girlfriend was coming from Las Vegas and it was time for us to move on. He was a very entertaining host, yet he kept to himself without imposing, just observing. While many doubted how devoted he was to the Family, the act of taking us all in made me feel his love for us. As we continued to brainstorm about what to do next, Makushla suggested we go to Maui. Inter-island airfares in those days were pretty cheap.

We landed in a comfortable vacation rental on the coast of Kihei, western Maui. It was desolate, dry, and hot. Only a sprinkling of cottages sat along the ocean, with a scruffy desert-like hill rising up behind us along the two-lane road that drifted off with no change in scenery for miles. A shallow reef came in very close to shore and ran along the coast. I waded through the water outside our door. As far as I could walk, the water level never rose higher than my knees.

I ended up spending my time sewing a few new designs I was conjuring. I do not recall where the fabric came from, but it was synthetic and silky with a flow you used to get only with bias-cut garments.

Some were striped, some prints, and some solids. Ancient Greece was my inspiration, and I designed fluidly draped gowns fit for the goddesses we endeavored to embody. Everyone wanted to wear one—there's nothing like a new dress to perk you up. The Council discussed developing my clothing line, Crabtree Creations, a way for us to make money, and pictures were taken of the dresses. But this was again to be placed on hold. Makushla decided we should go to the other side of the island, where we had lived on five acres near Makawao. She had dreamy memories of our waterfall on her visit there with Yahowha. So off we went to the other side, chasing a whim.

Tantalayo, Galaxy, Ahom

Makushla did not enjoy being in the position of making decisions or heading up the Family, but we nudged her into it. The Council found it challenging at times to agree on things. The three nursing mothers looked at everything from the vantage point of needing to be protected and cared for. They bore Yahowha's children and thus felt entitled to be considered foremost above the rest. The elders strove to make fair and equitable decisions, while the four youngest of us, all within two years of each other, basically just had to go along. They listened to us, and more often than not, tried to show us why our ideas would not work. Going with the flow was the way of survival; I knew I had to. It really didn't matter, anyway. We would stumble along until we found our way. Thus Makushla became the divining rod of the Council.

We had become dependent on the kindness of strangers, and I'm not sure how we connected to this place, but we found ourselves in a rustic cabin in the woods way above Makawao in Olinda. It was mainly used for marijuana growers to dry and process their crops. Its thin, plywood walls and unfinished floor were quite raw, but a large open space allowed us enough room to sleep on the floor together.

One night, I was awakened by a couple of guys tiptoeing through our slumbering bodies on the way to a locked back room. A few minutes later they tiptoed back out, carrying a long pole over their shoulders between them with huge kolas of dried pakalolo (marijuana) buds suspended in rows along the pole. Hypatia and I both peeped our eyes open, caught each other's glimpses knowingly, then retold the story to the remaining sleepers in the morning.

The land we used to live on in Makawao was unavailable and nothing further panned out for us in Maui, so we returned to the Big Island. It seems like we used that time so we could meld more as a body and place Makushla at the head so we could return to the Family whole. They welcomed us with open arms, and at least the Country Club was basically set up for us.

We rode up in a truck into a languishing, landscaped circular driveway. A large timber building with the appearance of a lodge and sixty-four acres of fallow and overgrown golf course behind it towered over us. I climbed the tall cement steps to enter an oversized, open hall with dark wood floors and a walk-in lava-rock fireplace on the right wall. The left side was surrounded by a ten-foot-wide screened-in lanai. A kitchen and laundry area was at the back. Downstairs held two locker rooms with numerous toilets, showers, and lockers to adequately serve the entire Family's needs. There was also a room that had been a bar but ended up being perfect for the Council. I rolled up my sleeves and began the cleaning process with my Council sisters.

We continued the process of adjustment to life without Yahowha. Like the rest of the Council, the Family naturally turned to Makushla as our new guide, and she had no choice but to reluctantly take the reins. We were all still in shock and just put one foot in front of the other to keep going, getting up each day to take cold showers, have our coffee, hold meditation, and use the keys Yahowha taught us.

This all felt doable and safe. Everyone had a comfortable space to be in, even if it was only a few feet apart from someone else. We had no bathroom problems, plenty of room to be outdoors and plant gardens, and no worry about close neighbors. A small utility shed out in the backyard was used for teaching the children. And this was important. One thing we came to realize about the area was how wet it was most of the time, so we needed indoor spaces to retreat to.

Several old golf carts were discovered in another shed that had been left over from the defunct golf course. A few mechanically minded Suns got a couple of them up and running, along with a mower, and they blazed a few trails on the property for some extra fun. The dirt under us was rich, red, and ran fairly deep. Some of the men dug mud pits like the ones we had on Kauai to take mud baths and commune with the earth. We settled in and continued to live in the now as much as we could.

The Suns' workforce began getting more jobs doing handy work and eventually construction. Joshua's bakery downtown was flourishing. He had acquired new accounts in other grocery stores to sell our popular whole-grain bread and dinner rolls. He added a glass case in the front of the bakery that held a display of assorted pastries of the day, where one could order a sandwich or coffee to go. Life was kindling anew for us, and the flame steadily grew.

The washing machines at the Country Club broke down after so much use and having sat idle for so long. It would take some time till we could afford new ones. As I liked to go out and see what was going on around us, I didn't mind being our laundress, which also gave me more control over the care of my carefully crafted clothing. I still lacked driving experience, so Hypatia was assigned the duties of going to town to do any Family shopping—and keeping me company. A new strip mall with a laundromat had opened next to the Safeway store in Hilo and became our first destination.

We wandered into the produce section of Safeway after loading the machines.

Hypatia said, "Have you ever eaten these?"

I looked at the dusky, big, red, scaly berries with wonder and answered, "No."

"I have, we had them in Guyana. They're called lychee and taste heavenly. They have a grape-like texture. We're getting a bag. We can put two loads of laundry in one, and I can buy things on sale, and then we can pay for these with the leftover cash. We can go sit out behind the laundromat on the curb, peel them, and pitch the peels down the slope." Hypatia had thought about this; her Scorpio mind had a plan.

I was eager to give them a try, despite the fact that their skin was hard and scaly, and they became a new passion! The store and strip mall were built on a hilltop, and Hypatia and I sat in the back and blissed out on the sweet, jelly-like texture and exotic floral taste of our coveted lychees.

Eventually, the Family bought a couple of industrial washers and dryers to replace the ones alongside the kitchen area. Nursing mothers now could do their laundry at the country club. After the acquisition, Hypatia and I still had to run the Family errands. The Council didn't want anyone to be going out alone. She did not like driving and often gave me the keys to Mertzy, our Mercedes, allowing me more experience behind the wheel. Mertzy had followed us, island hopping from Oahu after Yahowha died. We had bought the car there to drive Yahowha around in.

We carefully shopped all the little mom-and-pop stores in downtown Hilo, as well as a couple of bigger stores like Kress, and found out who had the best prices on slippers, toothbrushes, and all the other little necessities that our Family seemed to need in endless supply.

It was fun getting to know Hilo Town, walking up and down the quaint, well-kept downtown streets. My favorite haunt became Hata's, the fabric store along the highway across from the ocean. Run by a family of lavender-haired, elderly Japanese women, they sold Viking sewing machines, fabrics, notions, and all sorts of Japanese paraphernalia like kimonos, tabi socks, and straw slippers with velvet straps. I could have spent hours looking at all the unusual items from Japan while compiling a secret wish list of fabrics.

During morning meditations, we were still attracting new people who wanted to check us out. They saw a happy commune with a warm and joyful Makushla at its head and were welcomed if they wished to join us. They did not have to go through the powerful initiation of ego-busting that often occurred with Yahowha. But they became contributing members and turned over their worldly goods to live with us as productive Family members. They fell in love with Yahowha anyway and helped to continue his legacy. Alcyone was one of them.

Several months had now passed, and it was the late fall of 1975.

Alcyone had recently turned over a small but helpful sum of cash to the Family, and a new Viking sewing machine was purchased from Hata's downtown and placed in my care. This became the start in earnest of Crabtree Creations. I was supremely excited and dazzled by all the stitches it could make and how smooth its operation was. I no longer had to deal with the shared Family machines that always needed fixing before I could start a project.

The Council decided that Peace, a Sun who had experience as a tailor, could help me start the business. We shared our sewing skills, and he knew far more that I needed to learn. But Peace and I ended up more interested in exploring each other than we did in designing clothes. Yahowha had named him Peace as he held the most serene countenance. I had never been with a black man before and found Peace fascinating. His sable skin was smooth and strong, and his kisses soft and full. In fact, Makushla was encouraging the Council to get together with the Suns so they could connect and ultimately be more financially responsible for us. The men in the Family were beginning to get a little testy about being governed by the thirteen.

Then more obstacles arose for the Family. Someone came down with viral hepatitis, and it soon spread throughout our ranks, keeping the men from working. Makushla called it the Golden Spell. The remedy was rest and lots of liquids, including warm lemon water and vegetable broth, which was a good thing because most of us were not hungry. I was one of the last to get a mild case of it and slept for a week. My eyes and skin turned yellow, and I dozed through it. Unfortunately, some did not fare as well and were stricken for weeks and even months. It didn't help that it was rainy all the time in upper Kaumana and everything felt saturated. The cooler winter temperatures sunk into our bones. Yes, it was still Hawaii, but our blood had become acclimated to the heat and more sensitive to the slightest changes. We were all beginning to miss the healing rays of the sun and the cleansing power of the ocean. There were not many beaches on the Hilo side of the Big Island, and they were miles away.

△ ▽ △ ▽

The morning of November 29, 1975, began like all the others. We woke up to meditate, and a fire was lit in our lava fireplace to take some dampness from the air. We chanted, and Makushla did her best to remind us of Yahowha's teachings. We had bought her a harp she named Lyra-Ho, which she often played for us to calm our scorched souls. That morning she said she was going to try something different, but we were never to find out what that was.

The air became dense; I could feel a tension in motion and a rumbling, and then an energy wave moving from a distance. The ground beneath us began to shudder and built up in momentum so much so that it stirred us from our contemplation. Tantalayo was seated in front of me, and I watched as she jumped from a full lotus position to what seemed almost ten feet in the air and raced out the door. I found myself moving like lightning behind her with the rest of us in sync. In my head, this jolt was so strong that I pictured a giant crack opening the earth into a deep ravine. It was all over in an instant. The panic of the moment to get outdoors dissipated. We all stood around looking at each other before bursting out in laughter. That was different all right, completely unexpected by us all!

The 7.4 earthquake at 4:48 in the morning did take a toll on the island though, and damage swept across in its wake. Two people were killed by the tsunami it generated. Miraculously there was no damage to our lodge—or us. It had definitely scared me, although now I felt completely energized in the aftermath; all that energy had bubbled up into me. But it was over, and everyone was safe and whole, despite my urgings to go snoop around and try to find the imagined giant crack in the ground.

Instead, we found that those volcanic rumblings had stirred up more than the earth. A week or so afterward, Makushla commiserated with the Council about how we all missed being by the ocean in Lanikai. So we came to a consensus and made plans to migrate out of the rainy Big Island again.

The bakery was starting to take off, and the Suns were getting more work. While the weather became uncomfortable, the Family had been settling. And once again all of this had gone haywire. A small contingent of the Council flew to Oahu to locate a new stronghold in Lanikai. A large house was found toward the back end on Lanikai Beach, and it also had a good-sized ohana or coach house. We called it the Sun Palace in honor of how much we missed the sun. The rest of the Council soon flew over with a few others to fill the second house on the property.

I was elated to be back and could not wait to commune with that white-powder sand and crystal-blue water. After walking to the far end of the beach where the sand diminished, I dove in and swam to my flat island, the gateway of Lanikai.

It took several weeks for the bakery in Hilo to close down. Meanwhile, Joshua rekindled his connections in Kailua to relocate the bakery there. The rest of the Family slowly migrated from Hawaii Island as they found the money, which took several months. We rented a few more houses to accommodate them, but once again, we were crowding to sleep on the floors, laying side by side in those few houses. Many nights I opted to sleep under the stars. The Sun Palace boasted a large lawn area ten feet above the ocean. The stars dotted the sky forever, and the sound of the crashing waves lulled me into slumber. The sea breeze seemed to blow away the heat and drama of the past summer, so I did not mind waking up in the sea mist—at least I could stretch out a bit and dream.

But Yahowha was not there to share it with us. Still in our shell shock, we fell into a rhythm, trying to emulate how he would have wanted us to continue. We still awoke each morning with the rising currents of universal life energy to exercise, swim in the ocean, and greet the sun. Once again, we settled into a favored rhythm of life.

The Mothers of the Council governed all the day-to-day activities and problems, with Makushla as the tiebreaker. In fact, she continued as our figurehead, as most everyone looked to her as the closest link to Yahowha. We all held her in the highest regard; she was the grieving widow. It was true that all the Mothers were, but she seemed especially affected and tried very hard to be stoic. She carried a very calm demeanor. Still, even though she was Yahowha's Mother Angel, she was not Yahowha, and she had never wanted the position she had reluctantly assumed. Moreover, the Suns did not always feel empowered by the Mothers, whom they felt, emanated condescension. As Angels watched and continued to take care of the Suns, this became a recipe for a simmering stew that soon turned roiling.

Makushla recognized the rising discontent and during morning meditations tried to enact different types of activities to freshen us up. One day we gazed into each other's eyes. Your gazing partner was picked by drawing a name from a hat. It had been an exercise to bridge our separateness. Another morning found us swimming as a group to Flat Island. It did not matter that many of us were not strong swimmers, including the children. We gathered surfboards, plastic wash tubs, and kickboards, while Belle Starr and I, who regularly made that swim, led the way. It was a test of survival; we would help each other to make the journey together. But the thing that really did bring us together was music. We sang the songs that reverberated in our souls, dancing to the beat, trying to shake off the creeping, seeping negativity. Still, we could not dance and sing all the time. Reality was setting in.

Problems evolved, and trust broke down so severely that our Family stopped functioning. We no longer had the income from the Source Restaurant to rely on. The Suns were supposed to be supporting the women, but they could not completely support the Council. It was very difficult for them to get jobs, and the bakery could not support us all.

Moreover, we continued to hold clearly defined rules about our dress and especially our hair. We adamantly kept to the Ten Commandments of the Age of Aquarius, channeled by Yahowha, which remained the basis of our beliefs. The Third commanded, "Harm not one of your body parts either by neglect, food, drink, or knife." Even though the men could pull their hair back or tuck it under, their full, bushy beards were not a fashion statement and displeased 99 percent of the general public by then. The Suns not finding work had also been a problem while Yahowha was with us. We had all found it harder and harder to leave his presence after morning meditation because they were all so completely dependent on his words and unconditional love.

28

Threading a New Needle

Day by day, the Sun's resentment of being governed by the Mothers increased. They were ready to be Yahowha. "Leave the house of your earthly spiritual Father to do the work of your heavenly Father," states the Tenth Commandment for the Age of Aquarius. Their Angels couldn't help but echo their sentiments. With no one to turn to for fatherly affection, they were developing an attitude and were ready for the Suns to be as Yahowha prescribed.

Unfortunately, the Mothers simply could not emit Yahowha's compassion. We were all too busy trying to maintain order and our positions, which was compounded by our competing for the Suns' attention in what became a chaotic battle for survival. I was growing tired of always having to be on someone's case about what they were doing to make things better in the Family.

The truth was that some of the Suns did go out and make a living, bringing in green energy, but many could not. Our long hair and beards, our unique sense of style, and our mannerisms put people off. We were arrogant and thought of ourselves as the enlightened leaders of the Aquarian Age. We did not temper our interactions with the world outside the Family—or the Maya, as we called it. People on the other side of our fishbowl misunderstood us regularly. We lived by the teachings of our Father, who had lived outside in the world for a long time. We lacked his expertise.

Then there were the musicians. Some of them felt a sense of entitlement that they should be taken care of too, and they focused on their music instead of going out to bring in green energy. Yahowha had perpetually supported that, feeling it was only a matter of time before their records would start selling and they had to be ready. Then of course, the women were not supposed to go out in the Maya at all, except for shopping with a sister, while the Suns acted as protectors and buffers for them.

But it was different for the musicians. Tantalayo and Lovely began a new musical adventure with the band backing them, and they were starting to go out to the Honolulu nightclubs to drum up some business. This was deemed acceptable.

We were no longer receiving money from the sale of the restaurant because the new owners had gone into default. Many of the children's mothers applied for welfare and food stamps, but the single women and Council had no recourse. We were not allowed to work, and food, rent, and utilities needed to be paid for. Once the money we had was pooled, it barely amounted to enough for the Family to eat. We bought cheap big bags of brown rice to make everyone feel fuller.

One morning at the end of class, the Council in their wisdom came down with the idea that they should each have a specific Sun volunteer to help be responsible for their upkeep. This divided the Mothers and Angels even more. The Angels who had a man that worked were receiving so little as it was, and they had become possessive of their men. They did not want to share their meager earnings with the Mothers, let alone the attention the Mothers siphoned away. In fact, some of the Suns had more than one Angel and had to work twice as hard.

I found myself unpopular and agitated. My communication skills were failing. I was too young and had little tact or life experience; no one wanted any of that. I felt entitled as a Council member and pissed off that no one would step up for my care. This became a mounting issue as time passed. Frustration grew, the Maya slowly seeped in, and old habits crept in with it, sucking the positive energy out.

The only thing that continued to bring us together was the music. Djin and Hom, our Family troubadours, continually wrote songs with acoustic instruments close at hand. An audience within earshot was eager to listen, but the band had nowhere to set up and practice because the neighbors were too close for electric guitars. It was a test for them to hear us chanting in the mornings, let alone to be blasted by amplified sound.

As our old personalities returned, the parts of ourselves we gave up to Yahowha to be light-bringers in the Age of Aquarius disappeared. The parts of us who clutched onto doubts and fears returned. The struggle for survival was a losing battle. Yahowha taught we were beings of duality, having an animal nature as well as the god speaking within. When you are in tune with the harmonies of nature the inner voice speaks to you, as your intuition. When you are not, your animal nature takes over during times of stress.

My great escape from all the drama of our day-to-day challenges found me walking in the sand to the end of Lanikai Beach and swimming to Flat Island every day. I found that it also saved my sanity. Belle Starr joined me on the journey. We both had youth in common and loved to swim, and walking the beach every day healed our souls. She was a couple of years younger than I was and had escaped a life in Beverly Hills. She was the daughter of a well-known socialite whose father was a government bigwig.

While everyone else debated the way to proceed, we swam, erasing all that judgmental chatter as we moved through the water. Yahowha's legacy was in turmoil, and my heart had slipped its tether. The results of our swimming were transforming, but not with the original intention. Belle Starr and I burned calories, but we also burned off the mounting tension churning from the struggle to find even ground to stand on after Yahowha's demise. Everyone seemed to have a different opinion of the way our Family should continue, and it was starting not to feel right to me, anymore. I felt disempowered, and no one wanted to hear my feelings.

Almost a year had passed since Yahowha had left us, and my eyes were opening to the world around me. In fact, Cygnus's wide smile made me feel as if just the sight of me completely warmed his soul. He was boyishly handsome; his thick, salt-and-pepper locks had grown longer and waved over his shoulders, and his sparkly, blue eyes were magnetic and full of mischief. He now had a full beard too, having adopted more of Yahowha's lore. Standing a lean six-foot-four, he had been a bit fitter in his heyday, but gravity and too much partying were showing their effects on his aging skin. But he did not mind; he joked it off, saying, "If you want to dance, you have to pay the fiddler."

He was also twice my age at forty-two. I had gotten to know him a bit when he had invited the Council to stay at his house after we had been kicked out of the Round House, a result of all the hoopla after Yahowha's death. Now, I would look forward to stopping by on the way back from the daily swim I took with Belle Starr. He had an eight-bedroom, old-style beach house with a coach house attached to the garage where his business partner, Art, lived with his girlfriend. In fact, Hypatia and Omne had rented a room in Cygnus's main house when her mother came to visit. They stayed on after her mother left. And the mysterious Mr. Moon from Korea had a small bedroom off the kitchen. Mr. Moon did not say much as he spoke little English. But he was a keen observer, and I always felt him watching. He worked with Cygnus and Art in their Samoan business enterprise as the go-between with the fisherman. It was rumored that Sung Myung Moon, the Korean cult leader of "the Moonies," was his cousin.

Cygnus and Art were middlemen in a shark-fin scheme, and they were selling it by the ton. Believing it a delicacy that contributes to longevity, the Chinese paid $100 a pound for it. Cygnus and Art would travel to Samoa and meet with tuna fishermen, who caught the sharks that trailed the tuna in their giant nets. Once trapped with the catch, the fishermen cut off their fins, hung them to dry from the rigging, and sold them in port. I later learned that they threw the sharks back into the sea to die. It was a gruesome business, but lucrative, and a Sun making money was attractive.

Back: Lovely, Hom, Cygnus, Mr. Moon
Front: Horus, Hypatia, Omne

The chemistry between Cygnus and me mounted; we liked the look in each other's eyes. I was taken in by his charm and deference—he treated me much better than any of the men in the Family did. In fact, he listened patiently and was very attentive to my conversation, offering advice on how to handle situations. Plus, there was often an open invitation for dinner. He was interested in the Family's diet and asked me to come make him food a couple of times. As dramas heated up in the Family compound, I found myself needing someone to confide in.

With no Sun to sponsor me, I began to wish I could take care of myself—sew clothes or perhaps get a job—but that was forbidden. I poured my heart out to Cygnus with all of these concerns. As I could not buy fabric or do anything else to escalate my business, Cygnus offered to help.

"I have friends who would love to have you make clothes for them, and I'd like something myself. So why don't you just come down here and stay with me? I have a king-size bed to share that would be better than sleeping on the wet lawn."

It was like an answer to my prayers. "Yes! That sounds like a great idea!" I smiled wide, barely containing my excitement as I naively jumped at the opportunity. Feeling so squeezed out of the Family, it seemed like a natural transition.

Facing the sea, his bedroom had a small cement patio and a sandy path leading out to the beach. At first, the large bed made me feel like I was just sharing space, but one thing led to another, and we were sharing bodies in no time. It was all too mesmerizing—someone who cared for me, a new sex partner, and a space to live in that looked out over the ocean. It felt like a heavy weight had lifted from my aching shoulders. Belle Starr jumped at the chance to move into the small room Mr. Moon had vacated when he returned to Samoa.

And then the morning came for my turn to lead morning meditation.

Makushla had decided that the Family might gain more respect for the Mothers if we each took turns sitting in Yahowha's chair and leading our morning chants and reflections. This also gave us a platform to air what was on our minds. I had missed a few mornings staying with Cygnus, something I had never done before, which was heavily frowned upon, and he was not going to class at all. Words of warning had been issued to me by some that I should not get too close to Cygnus's fire or I'd get burned. The rumor mill of our clan was ablaze with my audacity. But I had never felt this so-called heat that I had been warned of. So now, facing everyone, I felt defensive. And after the chants, I began to spew my truth.

"I am getting tired of hearing all the little whispers and gossip about what I'm up to over at Cygnus's house. Hypatia is there with

Omne, as is Belle Starr, yet no one speaks of them! And, no other Sun has volunteered to sponsor me," I stated.

Jupiter spoke up; "I'll sponsor you." Jupiter was suffering some health debilitation, and eight women sat by his side.

I laughed. "Thank you, but how impractical. You have all these other women and no way to support them in your illness!" The room went silent for a few awkwardly long minutes.

Then Joshua spoke up; "Well, if no one else will, I will." It seemed to me he was dragging his feet and looking at the ground to see if anyone else would offer before finally saying "okay," but reluctantly.

I continued, "Cygnus was the last Sun named by Yahowha, so I don't understand why you can't accept him. This is my decision. I'm tired of all this nonsense, and I'm going to stay there. He asked me to be there and will take care of me."

There was a lot of murmuring, but no one raised another voice of objection. So like it or not, this did solve a problem, so that was it. Class was over, and now everyone began to disperse for the day. That morning, I did not even realize that I was rallying for a mutiny. The problem was that no one had joined me.

29

The House of the Sun Rising

Previously, I had only brought a few items over to Cygnus' house to test the waters: a toothbrush, an extra sarong, and a bathing suit. Now that I had put into motion this self-created tsunami, I headed straight to the large Council closet and began to collect the rest of the clothes I wanted to lay claim to. When someone left the Family, they were looked upon with disdain, so everyone immediately began to treat me like an outsider, refusing to accept my decision lightly. Leers and words behind my back traced my path to the closet, while Isis, the hatchet lady of the Council, followed me.

    She stood beside me at the jewelry case and stated coldly, "You are not allowed to take anything with you. It all belongs in the Family." The sharp stare emanating from her large, round, dark eyes was powerful, but I had had enough. Having already gathered my sewing machine and a few dresses, I continued searching for my personal teachings and mementos. Then I turned to her. Towering over this tiny woman, a rising empowerment flushed over me for the first time.

    I stared back in rage. "Isis, you will never *ever* again tell me what to do. These are my belongings, and they are going with me!"

    She was dumbstruck: no one had ever stood up to her. Having taken personal responsibility for being the Family gatekeeper, she felt she had a right to maintain order. It was a rule, no one ever left the with Family stuff, and most wanted to leave it anyway. She swiftly exited to seek Makushla and the rest of the Council to back her up, I continued gathering and packing my stuff. But I could hear them in the next room, and I knew how it usually went: Isis would gain Council commiseration. So I needed to move quickly to get out of there.

However, I was surprised at what I heard. "Isis, just let her go and take her things with her," Makushla said. It was clear to her that this situation was different. Up until this point, a few people had departed, unable or unwilling to live as we had now been reduced to. We had numbered about 140 but were now down to about 110. I was the first of the Council to defect, and I think they were not ready to let go of me so quickly. Makushla also had a soft spot for me, having been through what we shared in the early days with Father Yod. She also may have hoped I was not exactly leaving.

Hypatia echoed my morning plea. "I live there too and still come to class. What's the difference between her situation and mine? Cygnus is a good brother. He'll take care of her. None of the other Suns were willing to do that."

Hypatia always stood up for me, and Makushla was usually the voice of reason, so the rest of the Council agreed, much to my relief. I think they were a little heartbroken at one of their own breaking ranks. But it was exhilarating to take this big leap. I did not know what was to come next and did not care, as I felt so out of sync with the Family at this point.

Cygnus/Vern

The rest heard the details on the coconut wireless, and it was all everyone talked about. This did not sit well with Alcyone, a newer brother who had joined the Family during our time on the Big Island after Yahowha had passed. The money he had brought in had been used to buy me a proper sewing machine to fulfill Yahowha's wish that I develop a clothing line. He felt strongly that if

I left the Family, the sewing machine should stay. He also was with a new Angel and wanted her to have it.

A week or so later, after returning home to Cygnus from a Honolulu outing, I found Alcyone's hulking form perched on the doorstep. He had been waiting for me all day. Cygnus would not let him take my machine, telling him he would have to wait and ask me for it.

I was caught off-guard. The sewing machine was my one hope to be self-sufficient. But when I went in, Cygnus said, "He should have it. It's only right. The money used to buy it was his. You can get another one." This left me feeling bereft and kicked in the gut, but I returned the machine to Alcyone. It did sound like the right thing to do. What I didn't realize at the time was that Cygnus knew that this was an opportunity for his own grand plan to take effect.

I was cutting my ties with the Source Family to a greater extent every day, unable to face the further disappointment we held for each other. Hypatia still lived at Cygnus' and was a tremendous support for me. She was able to slither between the two worlds hand in hand with Omne, the Family Astrologer and photographer. Belle Starr stayed too, yet she still maintained her Family relationship. But I became an outlaw.

Maybe because of this, Cygnus and I grew closer. He assured me it was all over with his girlfriend, Cindy, who worked in Nevada, and I fell hard for him, especially as I had been so disappointed by the lack of respect from the Suns in the Family. It was a joy and relief to be with him, as he filled the void of love and attention that Yahowha had vacated.

My mother was elated when I called to update her and invited her to visit. The house was sprawling, and Art and Mr. Moon were in Samoa, so she brought Aunt Adrienne too. They had lots of fun hanging out with us on the beach. Cygnus was his charming self and made a good effort to assure her I was safe being with him. But she was just happy I was out of the Source Family and living a more normal life.

In reality, though, Cygnus was a chameleon. He was the life of the party and wildly popular with men and women alike. But underneath this generous facade was a man always looking to find out "What's in it for me?" His favorite book was Dale Carnegie's *How to Win Friends and Influence People*. He was well-practiced in the art of persuasion,

Psychedelic Wild Child

so much so that he made his plans seem like they were his target's idea rather than his own. He knew he would eventually reap the benefit.

As Cygnus got to know Belle and me better, unbeknownst to us, he began to hatch a plan. After hearing about Belle's family in Hollywood, he convinced her it was time for her to return to them. He would be the middleman to bring them together and called them to explain that he was speaking on her behalf and had persuaded her to go home. However, the only way she would do so was if we traveled with her, so he convinced her parents to pay for our airfare with the proviso that I stay with Belle till she felt more comfortable at home. He also negotiated a nice fee for himself as a reward. She was, after all, a runaway, and he would be discreet with her story and not disclose it to the press.

I was excited to be getting away from the Family for a while, and Hollywood was a place I was familiar with, felt comfortable in, and was ready to explore in a new way. Cygnus' brother, Sonny, lived just down the street from the Source Restaurant on Sweetzer and owned a neighborhood bar on Melrose.

Cygnus said that we would only be gone for a month or so. In the meantime, he left the house in the care of Art's son, Kurt, who had asked if he could stay there and promised he would pay the rent and take care of the place while we were gone.

Belle's family sent a limousine to pick us up from the airport and deliver us to their stately home in Beverly Hills. Her parents took Cygnus aside, and I observed an envelope passed to him with their thanks, along with his agreement to keep quiet. I was welcomed into their home gratefully but guardedly. They had their girl back, so that was initially enough.

Heaven, Me, Hypatia

We stayed in her old bedroom. It was decorated like an elegant princess suite from a movie scene. Her glamorous twin beds were covered in blue satin bedspreads, with more draped satin crowning each bedhead. A large adjoining bathroom and a stone staircase from a balcony easily accessed their huge backyard pool. Belle had two older brothers, but they were involved in school and were not around much. A brand-new MG Midget showed up at the doorstep a couple of days later, a sign that her parents were making an effort to let her feel more freedom now that she was home.

We tooled around all over Hollywood and Beverly Hills as she showed me her world, lots of big mansions with tidy landscaping and sprawling lawns. We would make trips to Nate and Al's Deli in Beverly Hills for lunch. It was strange staying in a home with a maid and a cook. I had never experienced this lifestyle; it was a little hard to get used to. Belle had no problem asking the staff for breakfast or tea, whereas I felt I was imposing.

After a couple of weeks, her mother took me aside and asked if I did not feel like I should be moving on. Feeling intimidated, I said I understood. I thanked her for her hospitality and called Cygnus, who borrowed Sonny's Cadillac to bring me back to his brother's condo on Sweetzer. How strange it was to be back in that neighborhood again. I couldn't face going back to the Source Restaurant even to check it out. I couldn't tell if it was guilt that I had left the Family or that I just could not face the ghosts it would recall. It was also weird to be in a tiny apartment after living so large for that spell.

Sonny was similar in stature to Cygnus—tall, slender, and handsome—only he had dark hair and eyes and a softer, more easy-going demeanor. Sensing he knew everything about Cygnus, I looked forward to getting to know him better. Meanwhile, Belle was making plans to go back to school. She wanted to be a brain surgeon and began taking the steps in her life that her family had so carefully planned for her all along. Cygnus had other plans for me.

Sonny was married, but his wife Carol had her own condo a few blocks away. I did not understand it at first and was told it was where she worked. They did not allude to what kind of work she did.

One morning in bed I was discussing with Cygnus what I should do with myself.

"I want to be a clothing designer. Yahowha always said that was my path. I'm good at it and have a passion for it. But I really need to make some money, and I need a new sewing machine," I reminded him.

Cygnus replied, "You should do what you do best."

In my innocence, I asked, "What do you think that is?" He pulled me closer to him, and things got sexual. Afterward, I pressed him more and asked, "No, really. What do you see for me?"

He said, "You really are good in bed and could make money at it. You know my last girlfriend, Cindy, went to Las Vegas and was making money hand over fist working at the Cottontail Ranch."

"That sounds like a bit much. I'm not going to do that," I replied.

"It's not much different than having sex with one of the Suns of the Family that you weren't in love with. At least you would be compensated," he said grinning.

So that was it! I had always wondered about Cindy, but in my naïveté had never asked. What Cygnus did not say was that once she got there and was on her own, she stopped sending him money, and his cash flow dried up.

Maybe it was the allure of the underbelly of life, the easy money, or just the experience—or my lack of it. I really did like sex; why shouldn't I make money from it? In the Family, I did have all kinds of sexual relations, and where had that gotten me? I actually did not have any other skills and could make so much more money than I would if I sewed or waitressed. The next thing I knew, Cygnus was suggesting that I meet with Carol, who would show me the ropes. And yet again, my hormones were getting me into trouble!

30

Running in the Fast Lane

Carol called me the next day. "You'll need some new clothes and some sexy underwear. You should also shave your legs and armpits. I can help you with your make-up." She had seen me dressed in my half-hippyish outfits and encouraged a makeover. Cygnus could take me shopping.

At this point, Cygnus was reverting back to being Vern. His brother, sister-in-law, and all his friends could only relate to him using that name. He eventually became Vern to me too, his spiritual persona now vanished in a puff of smoke, and he began addressing me as Dawn. He felt more comfortable introducing me to his friends that way.

I fell so easily for it all. They all made it seem like their lives were so glamorous. I wanted that. Everyone had such nice apartments, cars, and clothes, and no one seemed to want for anything. It was a huge departure from my previous life, with its few material possessions. I find it hard to make excuses; I just did it. With a new wardrobe and a little courage, I walked over to Carol's house and rang the doorbell at the gate.

She lived in one of those Hollywood-style apartment buildings built in the sixties with two stories of cookie-cutter apartments, one after the next, up and down. Twisted wrought-iron railings lined the outdoor hallways, and lots of palms and foliage were planted in front. She buzzed me in, and I wound my way to her apartment. Carol was all dolled up. Her bright-red hair was teased high with bangs and flipped at the shoulders, dusting her crisp, white, button-down blouse unbuttoned to show off her ample cleavage and a simple gold chain hanging there. Her buxom, curvy figure was highlighted further with tight-fitting, maroon bell-bottoms. I looked around and found that the apartment was decorated in that same sixties style: plastic ferns, Plexi "stained-glass" panels, and low furniture with simple lines. I could detect a lingering scent of Lemon Pledge, and Muzak played softly in the background.

"You look great! What a transformation," she said, waving me into the living room to sit down on the couch while she explained how it all worked.

"We have pre-arranged appointments of approximately thirty minutes each with plenty of time in between to collect and tidy ourselves—and to be sure that the customers don't meet each other. You get 50 percent of the take, and I take the other half for providing the client and a safe, clean environment. I'll also make lunch for us later. How does that sound?"

"Umm, okay, I guess," I said, feeling it all sink in and just attempting to go with it.

"We'll call you Donna. You never want to give them your real name. Also, keep things simple and just try to do what they want you to. Nothing unusual, of course. That always costs extra. Now, let's fix your makeup," she said and led me into the powder room.

It was the spring of 1977, and I was just shy of my twenty-first birthday, reeling from the turnaround my life had taken over the last five years. It wasn't hard; I fell right into it and ended up working at Carol's house a couple of times a week. I kept in mind it was all about the money, which Vern would ask for when I came home as he had spent most of the money he had received on our arrival. "We have to pay for our expenses staying at Sonny's house, and we need to save up to get our own place."

Vern found a little furnished apartment on West Hollywood Boulevard similar in style to Carol's, but it was in a much bigger complex and had a kidney-shaped pool. I thought we were going to move there together, but he said, "No, it's for you to work out of." He would remain at Sonny's house, and I would work at the apartment. He also found another madam to start sending me clients because Carol only wanted me to be an exclusive, "in-house" person. Vern made bigger plans seeing how easily I would probably go along with them. Why did

I never see this coming? This was not my Hollywood; it was one I grew more unhappy with over time.

But I did have some very tantalizing "Hollywood" experiences, like being a date for a porno theater owner at the annual X-rated film awards held at the Beverly Hilton Hotel. At the big bash, I danced with Johnny Wadd, feeling the voluminous length of his member rubbing me from behind on the dance floor. We ended up in a bungalow in the back, where people were having sex and cocaine was lying in piles all over the place. It was a scene out of its own movie. Another time, we went to a party for Vern's madam friend, and someone passed me a joint laced with angel dust. It was a déjà vu experience from my teen acid trip in Chicago. But I did not meet any magical people, just a bunch of soulless, pretty faces who would do almost anything for some more dope or a blow job. Somehow, I just seemed to float through these experiences feeling very detached from them, like I was just watching the whole story unfold before my eyes.

Vern tried to placate me. He would take me to parties and dress me up, filling my nose with cocaine, but it was wearing thin. I wanted to go back to Hawaii. Then one day, I went over to Sonny's in the early morning. I was missing Vern and wanted to surprise him and make breakfast. I rapped lightly on his bedroom door, turned the handle, and stepped in. There was a lump on the bed curled up next to him.

"Good morning," I said flatly, barely able to hold my heat.

They both sat up at once, staring back at me in surprise. Vern blurted out, "It's not what you think."

"I don't think you know what I think," I replied sadly.

Meanwhile, the young woman gathered up a sheet, wrapping it around her nakedness, and began making the motions of gathering her things. Trying to wrestle control, Vern told her, "Stop, come back to bed. Everything is okay." But she continued to gather, and I just watched them. As Vern stared up at me, I could see he was trying to come up with an excuse.

"She's just an old friend and was too drunk to go home," he finally spurted out.

"And the only place she could sleep was bare-assed with you," I sarcastically spit back. "Old friend or not, I'm not buying this. Unless we make plans to go home to Hawaii, I'm making other plans that don't include you."

"Okay, okay, I'll call the airlines and get it all arranged," he said. "I was going to, anyway. You're making this a way bigger deal than it is," he said jovially.

I smiled grimly and said, "Call when you have news," slamming the door shut.

This had not been the first time, either. Another woman from the Family had come to LA and found Vern. So he brought her over and suggested she move in with me and we both work from the apartment. That lasted for about two days.

I worked up the courage and told him, "No! This is what I left behind in the Family. I will not be in another multiple-woman situation!"

He suggested, "Maybe one of you could go to work at the Cottontail in Las Vegas."

I said, "It will have to be her because I am not going anywhere but away from you if she stays here."

So Vern knew that I meant what I had told him when I found him in bed with his "old friend." He called Hawaii to let Kurt know we were coming home, but there was a problem: our phone had been disconnected. He had a hard time tracking Kurt down, and when he finally did, Kurt told him he had not paid the rent on the house and had ended up getting evicted. All of the furniture and possessions from Vern's house, including all of the clothes I had from the Family and my teachings, were disposed of too. We had said we would be back in a month, and it was now more than four months later. I was completely heartbroken. All I had left from my Family experience was gone. When I ran into Hypatia sometime later, I found she had saved some of my teachings, and she returned them to me. That was something. I may not have been practicing those teachings, but they represented truth, honesty, and something meaningful in the time I spent with Yahowha.

We made plans to go back to Hawaii anyway, but it just took a little longer. I had to make more money, and we needed to find a new place to live. The longer it took, the harder it was. Sonny began getting tired of sharing his condo with Vern and all of the characters who hung around him. After all, Vern had many dubious friends, all making a living doing questionable deeds. Carol was also not feeling very good about us being there—and especially about me going off on my own.

She really held it more against Vern than me, but our relationship shifted, and she became much more superficial and not as friendly.

Then one day, Vern got some good news from a friend named Joe who had a house in Kailua just off the beach with a backroom we could stay in. That got us excited, and we bought tickets and returned within a week, leaving all of the mess of LA behind. I got off the plane, and the smell of flowers and salt air filled my lungs. The humidity filled my pores with a comfortable familiarity, and the colors of life were alive—unlike the colors of LA's media hype.

Joe met us at the airport to drive us over the hill. When we arrived at his place, the backroom turned out to be a renovated garage, now used as a laundry room and an extra closet, a long rod stretching across the back wall where Joe's clothes hung behind a king-sized bed. A beach-style bathroom with an entrance from outside led into our room. But we were back in Hawaii and close enough to Lanikai to feel like we were home.

31
Chinatown

Me and Vern, in our garage-closet-bedroom at Joes.

Vern had a friend named Pam who used to come by for parties at our Lanikai house and loved my clothes. She was closer to his age and had a strawberry-blond afro and a couple of kids. We had met a year or so earlier while I was still in the Family, I had made a dress for her, one of my off-shoulder caftan designs. She had worn it for Halloween, I guess as some sort of joke on the Source Family.

    Soon after our return, Vern re-introduced me to Pam. But this time, he introduced me to her like he had introduced me to Carol. Pam worked at a private "bath house" just off Hotel Street in downtown Honolulu. She looked at me with a sidewise glance, and I could tell she was wondering how I had made the switch to ditch the Family. Pam nodded her head and agreed to arrange an interview with her boss, a tiny Chinese woman named Willie, who hired me to work a couple of days a week.

It was called Furoya's, *furo* meaning "bath" in Japanese. Most of the customers were Japanese locals, sailors, or tourists. Pam and I would work the same days so I could ride into town with her. All the girls we worked with met at a parking lot at least a mile away from Furoya's. We would then be piled into an old Buick Riviera by Willie's trusted helper, "Unko," who drove us the rest of the way, his eyes constantly glancing in the rearview mirror to check if we were being followed. He sometimes drove in huge circles to make sure no one had tailed us to Furoya's rear entrance.

Willie and her husband, Unyon, ran a tight ship. Everything had to be just so, and she had a long list of rules. You had to have a weekly doctor's clearance for STDs or you could not work. You could not work anyplace else. You had to be very clean, made up, and nicely dressed. One night, for instance, she did not like my sexy beach cover-up and told me to change. Once inside, we were not allowed to leave till the shift's end.

Each girl was assigned a "room" on arrival, one in a row of cubicles fifteen feet deep by four feet wide painted a bland gray-green. Each room had a sink, shower, and a single, thin mattress on a platform against a wall. All of the girls congregated in a room once used as a kitchen, where old equipment covered with big plastic tablecloths created a barrier between the front and back. We sat in back, waiting at old, small diner tables and keeping ourselves occupied with magazines, cards, books, and conversation.

Unyon sat in the corner with us by the back door. He seemed ancient, but he was in his late sixties, always hunched behind his newspaper and peering over the top edge to keep an eye on basketball games on the TV hanging from the wall. His eyeglasses were Coke bottle thick, but he did not miss anything that happened.

Willie sat at the front of the room on the other side of a counter. Customers peeked over the counter to scan the room and make their choice known to Willie. She then showed them to a waiting area. If you were picked, Willie would sharply shout your name—and you had better be ready as she easily got in a snit. You would then take the customer to your "room," where they had twenty minutes in your company.

Unko picked up take-out food for us, often from Wo Fat's Chinese restaurant, which I loved. As Willie was always looking down her nose at me, I wanted to get on Unyon's good side and asked him what his favorite dish was. He smiled wide and spoke in a gravelly voice tinged in Pidgeon, "It's simple noodle dish, with char siu cut small, sesame seed, green onion, oyster sauce." He smiled and looked over his shoulder while watching me eat, saying, "It's very good, right?"

It was. I ended up craving Gon Lo Mein while working there and still look for it on every Chinese menu today.

One month, I brought in a positive result from the doctor. Being tested didn't stop you from catching anything, just from spreading it further. I had caught the clap from a Japanese sailor who had had the most unusual appendage. Slipped under its skin and dotted all around its head were pearls, a fabled Japanese aphrodisiac. I had heard stories about them from the other girls, but this was my first time ever seeing them. Somehow, I had sensed something was not right and was hesitant at first. But I got distracted by the fascination of it and did not listen to my inner voice.

The doctor's visit was another eye-opening experience. I was also pregnant! What a shock; after all those years of trying to get pregnant in the Family, here it was. I had no idea who the father was, and I had to make sure it did not happen again. Yahowha had taught us that the soul entered the body in the first breath at the moment of birth. So I was not killing a soul, just stopping the vehicle it could inhabit from completing. I did not have any problem making arrangements to get an abortion, along with birth-control pills to take later and shots for the clap. This meant I was unable to work for a couple of weeks, which I really didn't mind at that point. If fact, I looked forward to the time off. Working at a bathhouse was far from glamorous, and I hoped it was just a stepping stone.

Pam and I had become good friends. She told me which doctors to go to and often drove me there. She looked into a free class at the Kailua library to study for the GED test and persuaded me to join her in taking an English class. I graduated in the ninety-eighth percentile of the entire graduating class of Kalaheo High School, class of 1978.

Once back at work, it was harder to make money at Furoya's. Each customer paid $50, of which I received half. Willie controlled how many clients you saw. If she liked you, as she did the local girls, you made a good amount of cash. But the rest of us hardly ever saw the local girls, as they never emerged from their cubicles. Willie did not really take to me and only gave me a few clients each time. I could not be molded into her servant, and she saw me as hard-headed.

She commonly told the customers whom they wanted, and I would often get ones that were difficult or rude. In fact, I never had any regulars until Ted came along, a Japanese taxi driver. He began asking for me, and Willy would try to talk him out of it. But he would threaten to leave if he couldn't see me, so she let him. She wanted his money. Ted was crazy about me and would see me a couple of times a week if business was good. Around this point, Willie began giving me two customers a night, so I would go home with $50. Then she started giving me fewer.

Unyon didn't like this and told her to pay me $50 no matter what, even if she had not given me any customers. My friendliness had won him over. So she started giving me more customers—she was not going to give me something for nothing! But on a busy night, I would only take home $125, which did not happen often. Her local girls made twice that on a regular night. They went home to chase the dragon, as they called smoking heroin, to mentally escape their pimps.

I still couldn't get more than two nights a week, though, and Vern and I needed to get our own place because Joe's welcome was wearing thin. He was an alcoholic bartender in a fancy nightclub downtown and really didn't want roommates. Vern had heard about another place that operated similarly to Furoya's in the downtown industrial area, and I began working there a couple of days a week too. But I wasn't feeling comfortable with it all. What had started out to be fascinating had become trashy, and the allure of it had disintegrated. I could not get close to any of the other women, let alone tell them of my past. I found that if I let them, people would just talk about what they wanted to talk about and never asked me about myself, anyhow. I was working with women who had big issues: drug problems, numerous children with bad boyfriends, *real* pimps who were physically abusive, and angry, dangerous lives.

Nicki was another old friend of Vern's and had a successful "business" she ran from a downtown Honolulu high-rise apartment. She had a higher-class operation, with local businessmen coming over for some afternoon delight. She was planning to move back to California, so she made arrangements for me to take over her apartment and phone line. It sat on the twenty-sixth floor, with a spectacular view from the balcony that spanned from Honolulu Tower, across the ocean to Diamond Head, and up into the hills of the Pali. It was breezy and much classier. Finally, I could have my own business and would no longer have to deal with those grittier types.

While Nicki was "training" me to use her book and run the business, she introduced me to Dr. Dickie. You could make an appointment, give him a blow job, and he would write you a prescription for Quaaludes. They had become a companion drug to cocaine for me, helping to take the nervous edge off and make all my worries and inhibitions melt—which was especially good for sex.

Every day, I drove my second-hand (from Cindy) red Volkswagen to the Honolulu apartment Nicki had turned over to us. The telephone would ring with customers calling. But they didn't call all the time, and I often had to peruse the book of phone numbers she had left with me, trying to persuade some activity.

Additionally, the place in the industrial area was only offering me a day here and there, and Willie was still only giving me two days a week. I needed more money to sustain our lifestyle now that we had credit card bills and two rents to pay.

I was much happier, though. Looking out at that view from the living room couch cleared my head. I was making more money, but with our expenses mounting, Vern taught me how to apply for credit cards, showing me how to fill in all the boxes so nothing looked suspicious. It seemed that they rarely checked references, and I would scribble in "executive secretary for a big corporation" as my position, which apparently made me 50K a year. So the cards began rolling in, and I went shopping.

One day, Willie called and asked me to meet her at a public spot that afternoon as she wanted to talk to me. So I met her at a lookout off the highway, where she was waiting for me with a wily grin. She said snidely, "Unyon saw you one night at the other place. He often goes around checking them out for new girls, and there you were."

It was a week or so before Christmas, and she handed me a gift-wrapped box. "This will be the last time we see each other. I don't like my girl's double-dipping. You know I have rules about that." She did not even give me a choice; she was happy to say "so long" and hand me the gift. It contained a set of matched towels. I think she was trying to tell me something!

My return to Hawaii look

But then things started to smooth out and get better. I was making more money in my own apartment, and Vern and I could finally get our own place. We rented a tiny cottage behind a much bigger house off Kailua Beach that was closer to Lanikai. It was not a moment too soon, either, because Joe had a new neighbor, a single woman with a passel of teenage daughters. And guess where they liked to hang out?!

32

Pretty Maids All in a Row

Joe's house sat off a sandy driveway that meandered from the main road leading to the beach. Several older beach houses lined this rough, asphalt-paved lane between thickets of ironwood trees. A single mom and her teen daughters had just rented the cottage seventy-five feet from us, and Vern just couldn't help himself. One glimpse of this squad of teenage cuties hanging outside of their tree-shaded house entranced him to strut out and be Mr. Charming. He stood in front of the mirror, preening and fussing with his hair before he went out to greet them.

"Hello there! How lucky am I to live next door to you beautiful ladies?"

They responded in a chorus of giggles and downcast eyes and then blinked back up at him. "Where are you all from?" he queried.

"We're from Oregon," said Lacy, one of the older girls, and Vern flashed his big, toothy grin at them. That is about all he had to say and do to get them hook, line, and sinker. The youngest was thirteen, and there were five of them, ranging in age up to twenty-three, all dressed in shorty shorts with midriff tops or bikinis with cover-ups. And they were all very cute.

It took no time at all till they were all hanging out at our house after school. Joe didn't mind—he was a good-looking, fit, single, surfer guy, his thick, shaggy hair swinging over his eyes, and his handlebar mustache shadowing a wide, flirtatious smile. He was hoping too.

At first, Vern had them over only while I was downtown. He couldn't have been happier to have a teenage harem all doting on him without my glaring eyes. But this evolved, as things do when teenage girls need to spread their wings. They were cheery, bubbly, and full of drama, and initially, I deemed them harmless because of their ages. Soon, they became a part of our daily lives—the five of them, plus their girlfriends, compounded into a much larger group. Joe, Vern, and their buddies were tickled. I was not.

In the Source Family, I woke up very early for meditation and smoked my one hit of herb. Now I woke up later, rolled over, and picked up a joint left from the night before to help face the day. That day was not supposed to include other women vying for my spot.

My friend Ted from Furoya's had fallen heavily for me. A bachelor who lived alone in a rented room in Kaimuki, near my Honolulu nest, he stood eye to eye with me in height, stout but fit—not the usual slight Japanese build as he was Okinawan. All the features on his kind, moon-shaped face seemed to raise slightly from its flat surface, and his infectious smile was framed by his slicked, black hair scented by pomade. He was always ready with bad jokes to make me laugh at their corniness.

When he discovered I was no longer at Furoya's, he made a frantic search until he found me working at the new place in the industrial area. Cab drivers knew all the haunts. He was concerned that something bad had happened and wanted to help however he could. I told him about my new apartment, which excited him, and he started visiting me there. Sometimes, he would give me money if I needed it, and always if he wanted sex. I told myself that at least what he paid me was all mine. But really, he was not making that much and could not afford to pay as much as I wanted. Ted also persuaded me to stop working at the other place now that I had the apartment. So Vern began pressing me to get more from him, especially considering our impending move.

The new, little cottage we had found soon made it impossible to be at home. We had relocated from one converted garage to another. But this one stood alone where Joe's had a kitchen and living room to share. To say it was tiny was an understatement. There was only a bedroom, which was also our sitting room. And the kitchen was just a galley on the other side of a thin wall with barely enough room to squeeze past a small table and chairs. It led to a bathroom just big enough for a sink, shower stall, and commode in the corner. But as it was a few blocks closer to Lanikai than Joe's, we were at least nearer Flat Island. I resumed my swims, once again trying to clear my head, but alone and from the Kailua side this time, a shorter swim. I escaped often, sometimes spotting the girls marching down from their end of the sand on their way to visit.

The Samoan shark fin business became a story of the past, and since I had fallen into this scenario, it was now left entirely up to me to make us money. It had been so hard to leave the Source Family that I found myself afraid of being alone. I was also scared to lose Vern. I had become dependent on him psychologically since leaving the Source Family.

Soon, the little girls began playing on my nerves, and it became clear to me what had happened with Cindy and Vern because it was playing out before my eyes. When I came home from Honolulu, the girls were all hanging around the house, making Vern sandwiches and Ovaltine and keeping him entertained while they all got high on my dollar. I had fallen into an age-old trap, and it was wearing on my nerves.

Occasionally Vern made money selling cocaine. After skimming as much of the original product off the top as he could, he would cut it with powdered inositol to make up for the lost amount. He would use my money to buy it yet always considered it his money because it was made through the apartment he had arranged through his friend. This illogic began to grate as well.

The activity of people coming and going to our cottage did not escape the elderly owners, who lived in a big house on the beachfront side of the property. The wife was a drunk who often dropped by with a cocktail glass in hand whenever she fancied being charmed by Vern, yet she too became annoyed at this gaggle of little girls. Her husband was much less amused, and we were soon looking for another place to live.

Vern and I found a three-bedroom house across Kalaheo, the main road, further toward Kailua Town. You could still walk to the beach, but it was a long walk. Our new, little backyard offered some fenced privacy with a hedged, grassy area. Of course, the neighbor girls from Joe's followed us there too, continuing to dote on Vern while I was in town "working." But we needed to get a roommate; I could not afford to pay all the rent for that place and the apartment. So Charly decided to take our spare bedroom, also lured by Vern's entourage. He was Vern's coke dealer, a young Italian, tanned and buff, who would tool around shirtless on his motorcycle. His chiseled physique was good eye candy, and he had a friendly, charming way.

Meanwhile, I was spending more time downtown, partly because I had to make more money and partly to escape the reality of what was happening. The view from my apartment became my comfy little refuge up there above it all. Ted called every day to ask if I needed anything and became useful, picking things up and running errands so I didn't have to. And he was there for me when Vern wasn't. I drove home each night, but it was often into a situation where I just had to scratch my head about what was going on in my absence.

Vern was wildly popular with his men friends too and held bigger parties on the weekends. Those nights, I would come home after work to find his little entourage of pretty, young things and his thug boyfriends drooling for any tidbits Vern might toss, whether it be coke or his tales of living a life on the edge during the fifties and sixties. I did not like most of the people who hung around Vern, and I did not like watching them feed off of him and his big plans that went nowhere.

During the week, he sometimes got a ride into town, and we would go out to the nightclubs after work. Disco was just becoming popular, and though I was not crazy about it, we were at least socializing with other people. There was a funky side of disco that got my groove and reminded me of the black radio stations I listened to as a kid in Chicago. Plus, I liked to dance, but Vern did not, so he would dole me out to his friends as a dance partner, distracting me so he could flirt elsewhere. Vern also got me very used to having coke around.

Charly turned out to be pretty good as a roommate. He always paid his rent—without stories—and would loan a compassionate ear when I needed one. He saw clearly what was going on. His morning routine would take him on his motorcycle, shirtless, to get orange juice and who knows what else, his dark curls haloing out in the wind in his wake. We never really knew what he did or where he went, only that he peddled in small amounts of coke. He would come back after a few hours and then party on with Vern and his friends till the wee hours.

But one morning, it was different: he didn't return. Vern thought he might be hanging with a new local girlfriend. After all, we knew he was fond of teenage girls; it was one of the reasons he liked living with us.

Charly had been seen by our girls hanging out with some local teens down by the beach. The girls knew he had a thing for one of them. So with no sign of him the next day, we just figured it was unusual but maybe he was involved. And I had tagged along with Vern on many days-on-end drug parties with his friends. They would stay up for several days, talking bullshit and sniffing coke if they had a big stash. We supposed maybe this could also be what was going on with Charly. Then a few more days passed, and still, he did not come home. After a week, we became suspicious. But what to do?

A few days later, Vern called me into Charly's room.

"What are you doing in here?" I asked.

"You're not going to believe what I found!"

I looked down at him kneeling on the floor in front of Charly's closet. In his fist was a tightly rolled wad of hundred-dollar bills he had just removed from a balled-up sock. Then he picked up another sock, which contained a large, plastic baggie of coke. We both looked at each other with a knowing fear: Charly was never going to come back. I did not know what to do or how to feel. I could not call the police or anyone else to intervene, we were not exactly making a legal living. But Vern's concern soon turned into a big grin.

While living in Hawaii, you hear rumors of people becoming "shark bait" if they go sideways of the locals. We could only assume that because he was probably dating out of bounds, he was possibly made to pay a steep price.

33

Into the Dark, Deep End

Vern had developed a steady business selling coke now and had a contact in Chicago willing to ship us some via air freight. It was sent to my company name, Dawn's Creative Fashions. Yes, he had named it; I would never come up with something so droll, but I had felt his support of me superseded. Now, all we had to do was pick the package up at the air-freight desk at the airport. We got up early, and Vern drove me there in the little red Volkswagen along with his brother, Sonny, who had been visiting from LA. I hopped out of the car and walked up to the desk.

"Package for Dawn's Creative Fashions from Chicago?" I queried the clerk. He looked me up and down and said, "Okay, I'll go check."

After waiting for about five minutes, he popped out and said it would be just a little longer before returning to the back.

Soon, he came back with a suspicious brown, padded envelope that looked like it had not traveled well. He handed it to me with an unsure look on his face. It had been ripped open and haphazardly taped back together with masking tape—some of the tape ends curled up, having not even been pressed down. What to do? "Just keep on my mission," I thought. Everything moved in slow motion from that moment. I walked back to the double-parked car and got in, laying the packet on my lap. Not even enough time elapsed for me to tell Vern about it when the car was immediately surrounded by plainclothes cops who told us to stop and hand over the package. I did so promptly, with a shuddering "Oh, shit" thundering through my head! This was it; I would have to pay the price for Vern's bad business. I had no time to regroup and just had to go with this, even if under my skin, my entire body was shaking. A big, white cop with a paunch holding his badge asked me my name, and I told him.

He replied, "What is that package you just picked up, Miss Williams?" I had been using my married name from when I was with Pythias.

I looked up at him and centered myself, calmly stating, "Fabric samples. I'm a clothing designer."

"Well, we need to look into that. Step out of the car. I'm going to have to ask you to come with me." He handcuffed me, read me my rights, whisked me away to the back seat of a nearby unmarked car, and locked me in.

Okay, so I had sort of prepared for this. Vern and I had had a conversation about what to say if the situation turned south, but the reality was really hitting hard! Shit! I couldn't believe this was happening!

Then my old Source Family adage kicked in: "Be in the world but not of it." I had to remove myself from the situation and see myself as only an actor in the play. Outside the car, other cops questioned Vern and Sonny, but I could only hear glimpses of "I don't knows" and looks on their faces as if they did not have a clue what was going on. From the back seat of the unmarked car, I could see that Vern and Sonny were not being arrested. Vern had surely played the innocent, telling them he was doing me a favor by driving me to pick up a package at the airport. He had to say this in order to get away and devise a plan to get out of this—and get me out of this! I had to trust that he would.

I was taken to a downtown Honolulu police station nearby and placed into lock-up. After being uncuffed, I stepped into the cage to join five or six other ladies in various states of dress. Some looked like last night's hangover, some were in scanty beachwear, and all were from the depths of life. I think I intimidated them, and they just stared at me with looks of, "Who dis haole (a sometimes-derogatory term for 'white') chick?!" I sat down on an empty bench away from them in my new, beige, polyester wide-leg pants, silky Nik Nik flowered shirt, and chunky Candies platform sandals. The air conditioning blew cold, and I unrolled my sleeves and pulled my hair out of its ponytail as I started to feel the chill. They did not try to talk with me but just stared, so I closed my eyes and tried to meditate, hopeful that I might doze off.

I really wanted to sleep at that point; it was the only way I could escape the reality of this. I began thinking about asking for the prescription in my purse. I had been to see Dr. Dickie earlier in the week to get a fresh Quaalude refill. As it looked like I was going to be there for some time while they built a case for a warrant to open the package, I boldly asked the guard for my "medication" so I could at least sleep in this haunted place. At first, I was denied, but later they allowed me access to it. They must have thought it would loosen my tongue. After all, they knew I was only the shill and wanted a bigger fish. I thanked the guard, turned, split one in half, and popped it in my mouth, pocketing the rest. Then I lay down on the bench and gratefully fell asleep.

After an hour or so, a guard roughly shook me awake and took me to a questioning room. Vern had arranged for a lawyer, who was waiting there for me. A balding, middle-aged man looking sweaty in his blue suit, he seemed perfectly calm as he showed me into a separate side room to talk. I felt grateful that Vern had pulled through for me; a niggling doubt wondered if he would.

After introducing himself, he said, "They really made a mistake by not waiting for you to open the package and get your fingerprints on its contents. It's taken them a long time to get a warrant to open it." I felt a little easier knowing this guy was on my side. He then looked at me and tilted his head asking, "Are you high?"

I smiled wide and told him about the Quaaludes.

He smiled back and said, "Okay, you need to focus, be very careful, and be alert. We are going into the conference room, and there will be a number of people in there. They could possibly try to trick you, so under no circumstances—even if they open the package and toss it to you—don't touch it. Hold your hands back. Let it fall to the floor. Don't get your fingerprints on it."

I pulled my hair back into the ponytail again, trying to gather my wits as we walked into a drab-colored room empty of anything but a long conference table with metal folding chairs around it. There was no air conditioning in there. Plain-clothed cops stood huddled together in one corner, chattering. My lawyer sat down at the end of the table, motioning for me to sit next to him. I listened as the police joked about the package and what its contents could be while the effects of the Quaalude swirled through my brain. Only slightly nervous, I put faith in my lawyer—and the 'lude helped me ease up. I decided to have resolve, no matter what. They opened the package, and the large, plainclothes haole cop at the head of the table with latex gloves on exclaimed, "Well, what do we have here? Mother's little baking mix?" He held up a large Ziplock bag filled with white powder. I tried to look surprised, but not unbelievably so. I kept telling them, "I'm a clothing designer. I was expecting fabric samples, and if it isn't that, I don't know what it is."

He stated, "This needs to go to the lab for testing." They took a sample away and then all got up and left. My lawyer said I had done a good job and he was going to work on getting me out of there. Even though I knew what the lab results would be, it sounded like the cops could be caught in a technicality. I was hoping so! Meanwhile, a uniformed guard appeared to escort me back to lock-up.

A couple of cops returned about an hour later to wake me from my haze and took me to a small conference room to tell me that my package had tested positive for cocaine. Then they told me that it was only 40 percent pure and watched for a reaction, hoping it would rile me up.

I looked at them and said, "So what is that supposed to mean?"

They laughed and sent me back to the cell. A guard came to get me an hour or so later saying, "Lucky you. You can go."

What a relief! I jumped up, slipped into my Candies platforms, and was led out of the cell to retrieve my personal belongings. I opened my purse and found everything there in a tumble, but only four Quaaludes were left in the prescription bottle.

Astonished, I looked at the diminished bottle and stated, "What happened to my prescription? This was almost full!"

"Hey, that's what's there. I don't know. It's what you came in with," answered the smarmy guard. "Don't push it," I thought. "You're already in enough trouble."

I called Vern from a pay phone outside to pick me up, but he was not coming near that police station. He explained that he and Sonny had been very busy cleaning up the house and making sure there was nothing at home to bust them for. "Just take a taxi home. I'll see you soon," he said.

So there I was, still in a Quaalude daze, on my own as the sun set with no one to comfort me for my troubles. Another letdown. But I was a big girl and could take care of myself. Although I was tempted to call for Ted's company, I hailed a cab to take me over the Pali Highway and back to Kailua.

At home, Vern was on the phone, so Sonny briefed me on what had happened to them all day. The little girls were making dinner and waiting on Vern's every word—he had had such a hard day, after all. But what about me? I was the one who had sat in jail! All I wanted to do was peel off my clothes, get in the shower, and wash it all away. I felt overwhelmed with all of the fear and anxiousness of the experience.

The view from my lanai

After my shower, Vern came into our bedroom. "You did a good job, sweetheart, and I'm very proud of you. I think we might be off the hook, but we have to be careful. The house is being watched; there's a car parked down the street, and I'm sure the phones are tapped."

I was feeling as if everything might be okay. Vern seemed to think I had handled it all so well, but who knows what could happen next? There was a huge story here if we let them have it, but we were going to play it cool and act like nothing had happened, nothing was going on, and there was nothing to see.

I was too tired and confused to respond except to say, "I'm taking a nap. You can wake me for dinner." I just could not be bothered with anything else at that point.

34
Gasping for Air

Once again, we found ourselves looking for another new rental. We couldn't stay in this house, anymore. Sonny returned to LA, having had enough of life under a magnifying glass, and our friends stopped coming over—except for the little girls, who were oblivious. I continued to work downtown and felt fairly invisible doing so.

It was kind of weird how quiet our lives got. Word had spread quickly on the coconut wireless, and Vern had to stop dealing for a bit. He found us an unfurnished house at the end of Kailua Bay further from Lanikai. The further we got from Lanikai, the more nervous I got. It was my happy place, my security. The new house faced the ocean but had no access, only a cement patio where the waves lapped against it. Our previous rentals had been furnished, so we bought a big bed, on credit, and Vern somehow scrounged up a loveseat, dining table, and chairs. We sat on our beach chairs in the large, sunken living room. His friends slowly started coming around again when we felt we were no longer being watched and had not heard anything further from the cops about the package. My lawyer confirmed the case had been dropped.

I began to suspect some serious interaction between Sally, the youngest of the girls, and Vern. I saw her making big, moony eyes at him and remembered how that felt with me and Yahowha. No one could have stopped me. In fact, she bore similar looks to me except she was a foot shorter, with a peach-shaped face. And she was only thirteen. When I would come home, they were never far apart. And since

I had to work more to make more money, I was staying downtown more—and looked forward to it.

At least I had Ted, who was totally devoted to me and willing to drop by on a moment's notice. He still called several times a day to check on me. And I had other regulars too, some very happy I was there later so they could stop in after work. Although I was making more money, every time I would go home, I felt more alienated from it all, no matter how charming Vern was. When I would walk in the door, I would get the impression that the air changed once they saw me. The girls switched on their best behavior, the subject was changed, and they were not going to say what it had been. My resentment mounted, and I would make Vern ask for the money I made. I would not give it to him easily, explaining I had to pay for this rent or that bill.

One of my regulars stopped by one day several weeks after the bust. Bob was a local Japanese man in his late forties. I knew he worked in the police department; he had described it only as a desk job.

Bob looked at me with deep, sincere concern and asked, "How are you really doing?"

I replied, "Fine. Why? Is there something you know that I don't? Have you heard something about me?"

"Well." He drew a large, slow breath in and out. "There was this case that came across my desk, but I didn't do anything about it."

"What does that mean?" I answered in surprise.

"That's all. It came across my desk, and I didn't do anything about it. Let's just leave it at that. What I want to know is, what are your plans for the future? There are so many other things you can do."

That kind of surprised me, and I could tell by the look on Bob's face and his changing the subject that he was not going to talk anymore about it. So I just went with it and said, "I really need to think more about that. I've always wanted to be a clothing designer."

He smiled. "You really are so good with people. You should think about being in public relations." That was a field I had never thought about.

But now, I finally knew the truth. Bob was my friend and had watched out for me, a guardian angel in disguise. How lucky was I? Luckier than I knew. I was very grateful to him and still am to this day.

35

Twenty-Third Birthday

It was the spring of 1979, and my twenty-third birthday approached. Vern wanted to have a big party, as he now had his entourage, a new house on the ocean, and his life back. The day came, and the party began.

I donned a cute, new outfit, a modern, Hawaiian-print pencil skirt and camp shirt in black with red and blue hibiscus. I popped a black Greek sailor cap on my head and made a small spread of party food, crudités, chips, and dip that were barely touched. Instead, partiers were lured by the blow, the little girls, and their pals. Vern's thug friends showed up along with his club-buddy coke customers. No one was there to wish me a happy birthday; it was only an excuse to party. They were there for the lines to be spread out and to watch the pheromones fly.

My 23rd birthday.

The little girls arrived as a gang, along with several of their girlfriends, all giggling and wearing make-up and tight mini sundresses, short shorts, and glittery tube tops. Disco blared from the stereo, inciting the girls to dance. As the evening progressed, my awareness turned to the interactions between Vern and his teenage posse; he was mesmerized by them. He was not paying any attention to me. No one was, really, so I took half a Quaalude, realizing I was an observer at my own celebration.

As the gathering populated, I found it easier to disappear into my bedroom, preferring my own company, and felt another half a Quaalude would help. When I started to feel it, I wandered back into the living room with my camera and took a few pictures. It was something to do, but maybe I also subconsciously thought it would be useful to remember this event?! I saw one of the girls' friends, Nicole, slither into the beach chair next to Vern—my chair—and watched as she leaned in closer to him, all chatty and giggly. I reached into my pocket, another half a Quaalude slipped down easily, and I kept snapping away at this rude den of debauchery. But soon, I got bored of snapping pics and headed back into the bedroom for a while. Maybe I would do another half. I sat down on the bed, and no one bothered me or even came looking for the birthday girl.

Suddenly, I was shaken awake by a tanned man with a shaggy helmet of chestnut curls wearing a beige, three-piece suit. It was Vern's friend, Sal, who seemed very concerned. He was on a pit stop before going to the hot Honolulu restaurant and nightclub where he was the manager. An avid coke customer, he liked to giggle with the girls but was not a regular part of Vern's inner circle.

My head was spinning, and I was woozy but slowly woke from my haze, happy to see the smile bursting from his thick mustache. His dark eyes grew serious, and he said, "I didn't see you anywhere and was worried. One of the girls said you were in the bedroom, but you wouldn't wake up." He must have had an eyeful of the situation in the living room and continued, "I just wanted to make sure you're okay." Sal was no fool, and he was a gentleman.

"Oh, thanks. You don't need to worry about me. Vern has everyone else taking care of him. I'm fine right here, but it's sweet of you to be concerned," I said.

"Why don't you get up and walk around a little? What did you take that has you so knocked out?" Sal asked.

"Just a half a Quaalude. I would really rather be here on my own." I got up to move around a bit to prove my point, then plopped back on the bed, actually feeling unsure of my feet under me.

He knew what I meant, and he knew what Vern was about. I only wanted to melt into the bed and not have to witness it. I told him, "Really, I'm okay. I appreciate your concern. Go enjoy the party."

"All right," he replied, "but please be careful. Take care of yourself." He turned to walk back into the party but looked back and smiled with concern in his eyes.

I said, "I'm not going to do anything stupid. It's just that at this point, I'd rather sleep." And I did and still have no idea what else happened that night. I was not aware of anyone else coming to check on me, and Vern must have silently slipped into bed, unnoticed.

In the morning, Vern made no further mention of the party. The one good thing about having the girls around was that they were constantly cleaning, tidying, and keeping themselves busy, so I didn't have to. And I didn't have to witness the remains of the party to be reminded of it. Perhaps that was the way it was with Vern too: out of sight, out of mind. Vern's lack of interest had begun to make me uncomfortable, and I couldn't stop ruminating about the entire evening—what I could remember of it—and wondering what else had gone on. It felt unbearable. I had to get out of there and escape downtown, where I could develop my pictures and see what had happened. There was a one-hour service at Long's, so I'd stop there on the way.

When I got the photos back, I took a double-take of the images of Vern with his tongue down Nicole's throat. So *she* was his new fascination. This was worse; Nicole was at least of age. She was a thin, tan, surfer-type girl with long, flowing, sandy hair. This could be serious. I was gutted and knew that now, everything was about to change.

I drove home from work later that afternoon to find a little handwritten note in silver on burgundy paper on my bedroom wall. It had a cartoonish drawing of Nicole sitting in a crescent moon above a poem. This. Was. The. Last. Straw. Everything I had been bottling up exploded at that moment, and I became unhinged, screaming in anguish, "Noooooooooo!"

Vern heard all the commotion and came running in, demanding, "What's going on in here?"

"What's this about?" I shouted back at him, pointing at the picture. "You didn't even bother to hide it?!"

"It's just a sweet little note from Nicole." He was trying to brush it off.

"I don't think it's sweet, funny, or cute, and I'm fed up." I ripped the picture from the wall and spat, "This is not going to live on my bedroom wall. Do you think I don't know what's going on when I'm not home? I've had enough. I can't stand it, anymore. I won't be treated like this ever again!"

I turned to the bed and ripped my Egyptian-lotus-print sheets off of it in a furious rage, knowing they had been defiled in my absence. Vern grabbed me from behind to make me stop, and I spun and started beating on his chest with both fists until he was able to grab them and hold me still. That threw me into a further rage, screaming "Gahhhhh!" I broke myself from his grip and fell down on the bed, sobbing. "I can't play this game, anymore. I'm tired of being taken for granted and taken advantage of, of being your cash cow. You're going to have to figure it out for yourself because I'm done. How could you do this to me?!"

But I knew that he had done this to Cindy, the one before me. And every ex-wife and lover he had been with before her. We had all been duped by his boyish charm and "let's party" attitude. I ran to get a suitcase and began manically tossing things into it.

He watched me in surprise and asked, "What are you doing?"

"Moving to my apartment. I'll be back in a few days to collect the rest of my stuff."

He just stood there, staring with a confused look on his face, but he did not stop me. I could see the wheels spinning in his brain. He had to know this was coming; I could not have put up with it forever. Surely, he had a backup plan.

I packed up as much as I could and drove the red bug to my tower in Honolulu, where I cried for days. What was I thinking? How could I let this happen to me?

Aloha Vern

36

Regrouping

Ted stopped by to comfort me and make sure I ate, but I asked him to leave. I just wanted to be alone with my thoughts and my grief. There was so much to sort out in my head, so much to let go of. I spent the next several days singing "You're no good" with Linda Ronstadt and "Desperado" with the Eagles. Their commiseration was on constant rotation. I could not go out, so I lay on the couch, blankly staring out the windows at the ocean and mountains. Vern tried to call once in a while, but I slammed the phone down when I heard his voice and developed a new philosophy: I would rip my own heart out so that no one else could do it for me.

A couple of weeks passed.

Then Lacy called. She was an elder sister of the girls and a year younger than I was. "I can't handle being there anymore, either. Vern's attention is focused on my younger sisters, their friends, and now Nicole. You have an extra bedroom, and I bet you could use the company. Can I be your roommate?"

Ted

I was feeling vulnerable and, yes, a bit lonely, so I said, "Hmm, this could be a good idea. I have plenty of customers. Are you interested in that?"

She answered, "Sure. I'm going to need to do something to pay my way."

I hoped it was a good next step. She could see all the guys I didn't want to, and I could make a cut of that, I thought. She also became a sympathetic person to talk to. She certainly had had a front-row seat to the whole affair. And Lacy was fun. She consoled me when I was in desperate need of a friend. After all, I was not about to turn to my Source Family sisters; I would be too embarrassed because they had been right all along: I never should have trusted Vern.

Eventually, Lacy encouraged me to go out and play in the Honolulu nightlife again. "You need some distraction," she cajoled. She would find out from her sisters where they were going with Vern first to make sure we went somewhere else. We tried to have a good time living life on our own terms and escape from Vern. One night, we went to the new nightclub where they were playing punk music, and it cracked open a new door for me. I liked the sound of what I heard there. But otherwise, we would try our old haunts, where I now felt really out of place. So I started to drink a little more, always had a joint in my purse, and of course, resorted to my Quaaludes by the half.

Eventually, I gained the courage to call my mother and told her that it was all over with Vern and that I'd found an apartment in Honolulu. Her wheels began spinning. She was overjoyed to hear my news. She did not know how I made money (although she suspected) and said, "Maybe you should come home for a visit."

This sounded like the break I needed. Lacy could take care of the apartment and any johns that phoned in, so I was game. My mother was too. She was determined to reel me back in, and a new wave of excitement in Chicago could do it.

Within two weeks, I was on a plane to Chicago to spend the Fourth of July and my mother's birthday with her, and got very excited about what could be in store for me there. I truly was over all of my dark Honolulu adventures. Vern had shown me a side of life I never wanted to visit again, and at this point, I was mostly over him, so I was hoping to find some inspiration to help me move on to the next chapter of my life.

It was the end of the seventies, and the disco days were on their last call. In Chicago, I found a whole new energy running through the social strata. Punk rock was the antithesis of disco. After becoming so disillusioned by the whole scene in Honolulu, I found this new one refreshing. Its sound was raw, pulsing, and full of anarchy—and so was I. After being in the Source Family, where everything was love except when it was not, followed by the escapism of getting high and dancing to the disco beat, I was happy to have an outlet for the angst I had acquired. Finally, I came to the realization that I needed to rebel against others dictating to me and take my power back.

△ ▽ △ ▽

My sister, Amy, worked in a new store called Fiorucci's, which had opened in Water Tower Place on Michigan Avenue. The retailer originally sold wild disco ware from Italy; it was now geared more toward punk and the coming trend of New Wave. They made the best-fitting skinny jeans, stocked blazing-colored Barone make-up from Italy, and sold jewelry, shoes, boots, purses, and toys of all kinds. Everything exploded in bright colors or black—all in the style of the moment. They even had an espresso bar. Wild, new music blared from the speaker system, and employees would often break into frenzied dance sessions, entertaining the customers at any given time.

It was *the* happening place to work. Amy had to audition for the job, which was an unusual affair. People lined up to sing badly, recite dark poetry, do performance art, and in Amy's case, go onstage, introduce herself, and start talking about anything while looking adorable in her fifties thrift-shop dress with vintage sunglasses and spike-heeled shoes. Her curly, blond hair, blue eyes, red lips, and busty décolletage got her the job. Everyone liked Amy.

She brought me to Fiorucci's to meet her friends, anxious to make an impression and distract me from Honolulu with this exciting new chapter in Chicago. I desperately needed that. We went out to punk nightclubs, and I looked up old friends and made new ones. She and my mother worked hard to lure me into new sources of interest, hoping I would move back. It began seeping in.

I met several men who were much more attractive and interesting than Vern could ever be—and more my age. For the first time, I was interested in my peers and what they were doing, not intimidated that they might have something over me. I was now much surer of myself.

Dawn Hurwitz

We were all seeking the answers to something new, and punk rock and its rebellious edge was just how I felt. I was primed.

One day at Fiorucci's I ran into my old pal, Pat Day, working security. Pat had been a friend from the hippie days of Lincoln Park many moons ago. He was talking with a very alluring man, Paul Kirst. Both were giants, over six-foot-four. Paul resembled a satyr; his crown of long, blond curls and impish smile turning up one corner of his mouth made me want to dive into him. I could see that Paul found me equally as attractive.

He jumped right in and asked, "How would you like to go to see the Cars at the Aragon Ballroom tonight?"

Not wanting to seem too anxious, I waited for a moment and said, "I would very much like to see them. That would be great. Can you pick me up?"

Paul's elvish, blue eyes began twinkling. "Sure, give me your address. I'll be there around eight."

He showed up at my parents' house in his vintage, beige Avanti sports car. When he rang the bell, I was ready and went out to meet him. I was excited: he was so sexy, wearing tight, low-cut jeans and a checked, blue shirt unbuttoned to show off a set of curious beads around his neck.

In the car, we chattered with small talk. I asked him, "What do you do for a living?"

"I'm involved in several different things. I caretake a boat in Belmont Harbor and am involved in a few other ventures." With a raise of his eyebrow, he said, "It's better that you don't know."

Another bad boy. Well, how irresistible is that?!

"So, what were you doing in Honolulu for all those years?" Paul asked me.

Paul

"I wasn't in Honolulu the whole time. It started in Los Angeles." And I gave him an abbreviated version of my Source Family adventure.

I was not ready to reveal my life with Vern and the sordid road I had tagged along on.

I changed the subject back to him and asked, "What's with the stack of hippie beads around your neck?"

Paul said, "I follow a Voudon priest named Ordoon. I'd like you to meet him. I think you would get a kick out of him."

"What is Voudon all about?"

"I'll let that be a surprise."

"Okay, well, if it's something you believe in, I want to meet him," I answered, thinking I had been with Yahowha, so nothing would surprise me.

He made the arrangements for a few days later, picked me up, and said, "We have to stop at the grocery store first. There's something we need to bring him."

I followed him into the produce department at the store. "I'm glad you have a big purse because you have to steal a coconut." He quipped.

"Why do I have to steal it?" I laughed in disbelief.

"Because it's part of the ritual," he answered.

We stood in front of the pile of coconuts with Paul at my back. I unzipped my Fiorucci purse, a plastic, multi-colored beach ball on a rope, and managed to slide the small, husked coconut into it without being seen. We bought some sodas and continued on our way, laughing.

Paul smiled at me as we got back in his Avanti and said, "I didn't think you were going to do it."

"There's still much you don't know about me," I smirked, as we drove off to meet Ordoon.

The Avanti pulled up to an old theater building. It was not much to look at from the outside, just a big, three-story, brown-brick hall with glass-block windows. But inside, the walls were adorned with huge, brightly colored murals of Egyptian, Atlantean, and metaphysical themes accented in gold and silver. Okay, this felt familiar.

We wound through the galleries till we came to a closed office door, its window pane covered with opaque pebbled glass. Paul knocked on the door, and a soft male voice answered, "Who is it?"

"It's me," Paul replied, and the door opened instantly.

Sitting in a dark room decorated with old fishnets, African fabrics, and giant seashells was a thin, pale, older white man with long, greying dreadlocks and beard. There was something unclean about him, and a dry mustiness filled the air under the scent of burned-out incense. His rumpled jeans were topped with an African caftan shirt. He looked up at Paul, and I could detect a wanting in his eyes. He then turned to me and asked, "Would you like to have your Tarot cards read, or shall I read the bones?" He seemed to know we were coming.

"I can read my own cards. How about the bones? I've never done that before," I claimed with only a little trepidation. What in the world was this about?

With a curious smile, I sat down at the desk he gestured to with his hand. Paul informed me in advance to hand him the coconut when we arrived, and Ordoon grinned ever so slightly and placed it unceremoniously on the floor by his feet. From under the desk appeared a leather-covered canister containing cowrie shells and bones, maybe chicken legs. He asked me to shake up the canister and hand it back to him. He spilled the contents and spread them out across an African cloth covering the desk.

Making *um* and *ah* sounds like he was discovering something, he said, "You have been on a long journey and have a strong guardian angel watching you." He cocked his head in thought but said no more.

The guardian angel was so strong that it seemed he was unable to read anymore. "Hmmm, maybe Yahowha," I thought. He would surely watch over me. Ordoon stood and motioned for me to follow him into a large, empty hall with a stage, an altar, and more murals along the walls. Paul stayed behind with the bones, while Ordoon motioned for me to sit down on a big, ornate, wooden, Egyptian throne, the only piece of furniture in the room, and left me there to ponder the ancient depictions of gods in sexual situations on the walls. He soon returned with the coconut on a platter, halved open with a pile of its shreds alongside it and a small glass cup of its water.

He stated somberly, "I need to have a talk with your guardian and need your permission to do so." As he set the plate down on the ornate altar on the stage, I nodded. He then began chanting in a language I did not understand while playing a gong. This continued for about twenty minutes, at which point he stopped and said, "This is not working. Your guardian is too powerful." He then stalked off to talk with Paul and left me there alone. Honestly, I was disappointed. There were no explanations, and I had been expecting a little more excitement for all

Psychedelic Wild Child

that pomp and circumstance. Paul soon appeared, took my hand, and lead me out to the car.

"What happened?" I asked.

"Oh, nothing," he uttered offhandedly.

"Wait a minute. He had to have said something after all of that?" I returned, welling with frustration for the effort. Paul had to tell me something more than "Don't ask; it's better you don't know." I had done this to get to know him better, and we had just hit the wall.

He looked at me, raised an eyebrow and the corner of his mouth, and said, "Ordoon said I should stay away from you. That you won't be good for me."

I burst out laughing. "That coming from him is hilarious. He couldn't even get a read on me. And by the way, I could see the way he looks at you. I think he has a crush on you!"

I thought Paul, rebel that he was, had decided to take it as a challenge because we did not stop seeing each other, and I spent the rest of my time there on adventures with him. One was to a cemetery, where he grew pot in a little forested area. Another was a long drive to the nation's capital to drop off a large, heavy suitcase in a motel room, leaving the keys in an empty cigarette pack under a pile of leaves on a street corner of a residential neighborhood. We flew back on a small airliner and joined the mile-high club while wedged into a tiny bathroom.

Regardless of the eerie experience with Ordoon, I was still very attracted to Paul. During the heat of summer in Chicago, the harbor was a cool place to be. We rocked his boat whenever we could.

Paul & Pat

37

Checkmate

I had spent almost a month in Chicago, and when it was time to return to Honolulu, Mother asked me, "What are you planning to do?" At this point, I was not entirely sure, but after having a taste of this new life, my experience with Paul, and looking back at what I was about to face, the choice was easy.

She could sense my ruminations and knew I was having a good time there, so she said, "You can have your old room back, and I'm sure you can get a job. Why don't you come home? As a matter of fact, why don't I come with you to Honolulu and help you pack up? I'll even pay to ship your stuff back to Chicago." She wanted damage control. It was a ripe moment and impossible for me to refuse the offer.

The long flight back to Honolulu was full of fitful anticipation of my past and thoughts of a bright, new future. I had three weeks to complete this new mission. Dominating my thoughts quite a bit were Paul's beautiful, mischievous face and the ideas of what was I going to do when I returned to Chicago. I did not know how I was going to do it, but I really wanted to realize my dream of being a clothing designer. I needed to get a job—no one was going to finance my dreams—but at least I had a home base. Mother sat next to me, chattering on about anything that came into her head: the food she was going to eat in Hawaii, the beaches we were going to visit, the places here and there we would see—all the time avoiding the one subject I did not really want to talk about. Vern.

I had maintained a silence with Vern while I was away, but I did call Lacy a couple of times, who reported no news. She picked us up from the airport and on the ride home filled me in on other little tidbits of things that had happened while I had been away. While she was going through the list of who-is-doing-whos and whatevers, a bigger item popped out.

"Oh, by the way, Vern lost the house because he couldn't afford the rent, anymore. He moved into an apartment two floors under us."

"Really?!" I gasped. "You didn't think that was big enough news to let me know?"

"Well, um, I guess I could have mentioned it," she commented in an offhand yet suspicious way.

"How on earth did he get into our building? How did he know there was a vacant apartment?" I sputtered.

"I don't know. I guess he read it in the classifieds," she sheepishly answered.

I turned to her, dumbfounded. "Lacy, do you really expect me to believe that this is a coincidence?" I asked, shaking my head in disgust.

Lacy became somber. "I'm so sorry, Dawn. Vern made me promise not to say. I saw an ad on the bulletin board of the building and told him. He really wants to try to make up with you. He wanted it to be a surprise. Please forgive me. I can see how mad you are." She was almost in tears.

Mad was not the beginning of it. "Lacy, I do forgive you." I needed to keep my cool at this point. I also wondered what else she was not telling me. "I really wish you would have told me. It certainly is a surprise, just not a good one."

Mother sat in the back seat taking silent mental notes—very unlike her.

So, Vern was scheming on how to lure me back into his life. I was having the hardest time visualizing him sleeping in a bed two floors beneath my own, and thoughts of revenge seeped into my mind.

When I got back to the apartment, I kept up my wall with him and would not answer the phone. He did not try to come up and see me, either; part of his plan was to make me come to him. I was sure Lacy had filled him in on all of my comings and goings. I did not tell her initially that I was leaving because I was not sure where her loyalties lay. Now I felt even more empowered to realize my plan.

Mother enjoyed being in Honolulu and kept me busy running around everywhere doing errands and sightseeing. I ordered some moving boxes and arranged with a shipper to retrieve them after they were packed. Then it was time to let Lacy know, as I had decided to trust her. She was excited for me and really felt good about what I was doing. Plus, she was sincerely sorry for not having told me. Having become used to the business while I was away, she also liked the idea of screwing over Vern and promised to keep my secret, possibly feeling a guilty obligation to make it up to me. I made arrangements for her to take over the business and just gave it to her. I only wanted out.

On the day the shippers were to come, I called Vern. "We need to talk. Would you come up in a little bit so we can speak face to face?" I had had the month away and almost two weeks of building up my inner strength to do this. I was ready for him.

When he arrived, Mother and Lacy stayed in the back bedrooms to give us some space in the living room. He was all charming smiles and gestures, wearing the loose, orange cotton shirt and pants I had made for him as he sat down on the couch. He was all set to conjure me back under his spell.

I sat down, and he scooted closer to me. I just looked out at that beautiful view of Diamond Head. I was going to miss it, but I was breaking out of that tower, and my engines were revving. Looking around the apartment, Vern began noticing the thinned-out furnishings at just about the same time there was a knock at the door. The shipping company had arrived. I jumped up to answer it and showed the man with a dolly in, who asked me where the boxes were that had to be shipped. Vern visibly stiffened as I pointed to the stack by the open bedroom door. "Those five over there."

When Vern realized what was about to happen, the expression on his face paled, and he shifted from Mr. Charm to shock and disbelief. Checkmate, Vern. You lose. What an empowering moment!

I turned to him in my newly revived empowerment and explained, "While in Chicago, I had time to reflect on where I've been and where I'm going. You don't fit into my plans. I'm going to make something of myself, by myself. I'm letting Lacy have the apartment. By the way, all of the furnishings are mine, I earned the money to pay for it all. I'm leaving the large things like the couch, bed, and coffee table, for Lacy—anything too large to pack that can't ship easily."

He gulped and muttered, "No, these things are all mine." He couldn't believe what he was hearing, still sadly clinging to the belief that he had set me up in the business he had bought from his friend—with my earnings—yet he was somehow entitled to the proceeds.

I instantly retorted, "No, welcome to the real world. I'm taking what's rightfully mine, and there's nothing you can do or say about it to twist the truth. The movers are here, and it's all packed up and leaving. I asked you up here to say goodbye. It's truly all over now."

My eavesdropping mother suddenly appeared from the bedroom at this point with a shit-eating grin on her face. She greeted him in a sickly-sweet tone. "Hello, Vern. How nice to see you again."

"Hello, Audrey," he fitfully responded with a knowing, nervous sneer.

Mother opened the door for the man with the dolly now stacked with two of my boxes as he said, "I'm just going to stack these by the elevator. I'll be right back." She was so gleeful at this moment and could hardly contain herself, so she went to the kitchen to be distracted. I could see she was very proud of how I was handling Vern, giving him his comeuppance. I could also see Vern's thoughts in a whirlwind pinging around in his head. He could never hide what he was thinking from me. I immediately sensed that a fuse was lit, and he was about to explode.

Without missing a beat, I said, "I need to deal with the movers. Thanks for coming up to hear what I had to say." Then I calmly stood up and motioned him to the door. He slowly got up and walked out.

That was the last I saw of Vernon Gentry Van Hecke.

Dawn & Vern

38
Aloha, Honolulu

Mummy & Me on my lanai

Saying goodbye to Honolulu was a complicated issue. First, I was saying goodbye to my life in Hawaii, having spent the better part of the last six years making it my home. My heart was certainly in pieces over this. The Source Family was a no-brainer. I was happy to leave the downward spiral they were descending into and not have to watch it all disintegrate. We had all been there for Yahowha, for the unconditional love he had bestowed on us, and for the wisdom that constantly flowed from his soul. But when it came down to it, we had not been able to translate that to each other. Instead, I had managed to

Psychedelic Wild Child

jump into my own downward spiral, thank you very much! I would take responsibility for my own decisions from there on out, but I did miss the camaraderie, trust, companionship, and life with those of like mind. We had certainly looked out for each other . . . until we did not.

Then I had somehow jumped the polarity: Yahowha on one end, Vern on the other. I wanted some life experience. Okay, I got it. And there was a huge takeaway from this venture, one I would never visit again. I had learned about my personal power, how much I had, and what I could do with it. I could give it away, or I could make something for myself. Finally, I chose the latter.

So far, I had only seen a glimpse of a new life in Chicago, but the future was magnetic. I was the right age and in the right frame of mind, and some new muse had taken up residence in my psyche to inspire me and show me confidence. Feeling this new impetus was exciting, and my creative juices bubbled up, waiting to overflow. I was ready and primed. A clean page awaited. I knocked, and all the doors popped open. I was no longer afraid of what was to come, how I could fall, or how I could fail. Mother encouraged my creativity and kept me safe and on her radar, making sure none of this would ever happen again. I think she had learned a few new tricks too, and was there to gently guide me back to sanity. Of course, my sister was there to egg me on, while my father paid for me to get out.

I had come so far, and I was feeling the loss of Yahowha and the Source Family, the friends I thought I had found and now lost. I knew my experiences with them would always be a special time of my life, and I would now keep them sacred in the silence of my heart, where no one could ever ruin them for me. So I made a conscious decision not to speak about my past unless it was with someone whom I knew and truly trusted—and only if they asked.

During the short time I had lived alone in the apartment before Lacy moved in, I ran into some Source Family members at the last-ever Bob Marley Concert, held at the Waikiki Shell. They shunned me—literally—with their noses in the air, except for Sol Amon and Galahad, two boys who must have been about seven by then. They were tagging along at the end of the Source parade, and I saw the recognition and love in their eyes, and they saw mine.

I was on a date with a fellow I had met, a marine biologist, and was stepping out of my comfort zone to try dating and remember what a normal life was like. Tall, muscled, and handsome, he had short, dark curls framing his bespectacled, serious face, and I liked the curiosity in his eyes. He had ridden us there on his motorcycle.

As we walked to find our seats, he remarked, "Look at that trail of people! They look like they're in a play or something right out of the Bible!"

One of the stalwart Suns of Yahowha, Waterfall, who was the first Source Family person I'd met, was in their lead, wearing a robe with his long, golden hair and beard blowing in the breeze. Wearing their bright, aloha colors and flowing velvets, his entourage of women and children clustered in his wake, along with a few other Source people in tow.

"Yes," I reminisced softly, "I know these people. It's a long story. Maybe I'll tell you about it sometime."

He nodded with a questioning look but didn't pry. Bob Marley was taking the stage, and we still had seats to find. It was a good thing there was a concert to distract my date because I was not ready to share that story.

We found our seats, and the reggae beat blanketed the crowd, who moved with it like surfing a wave. Then, I sensed something moving on the ground under our bench and looked down to find two blond, shaggy-haired little boys rolling on the cement beneath the benches we were perched atop the backs of.

"Sol Amon," I urged, "Keep that umbrella closed. Galahad is right behind you! You might poke him in the eye or something."

He gazed up at me with a laser-zap soul connection. I could detect in the depth of his ocean-blue eyes how much I meant to him, how much he missed me, how much he loved me still. They were burning with the question, "Where have you *been*?!"

My friend looked over, surprised, and said, "You know these kids?"

"Yes. They're part of that long story I might tell you one day. Sol Amon, Galahad, maybe your parents are wondering where you are. Perhaps you should go find them?"

It ripped at my heart to send them away. In the old days, I would have taken Sol Amon on my lap and giggled with him. The compassion and love Sol extended to me was our bonding, so the synchronicity of the moment speared my core.

Today, I am still his Auntie Dawn, and we have a stronger connection than ever. And my date? No, he never heard that story. I would never tell anyone the story until now. Maybe a few heard bits and pieces, but I have not found many in my life I could trust with the whole thing. Who would have compassion for what I had gone through? Who would not berate me as my date eventually did? Because he heard a different story. He had found out about my business through Lacy, who answered the phone one day and said I was not home but she was available. "Available for what?" he asked her. She tried to seduce him over the line, and he felt betrayed. He could not go with a girl like me! This singed but did not leave a mark. It only accentuated the truth. I could not be a girl like me, anymore. I had to make some drastic, solid changes. If that meant I had to leave Honolulu to accomplish them, that was what I had to do.

△ ▽ △ ▽

Then there was the disappointment of Vern, of how he had taken advantage of me and used me to his own ends. Lost little puppy he was, growing up in the illusion of Hollywood before a stint as a sailor in the fifties. But he just could not break the pattern and only wanted to party, make whatever escape he could, and find someone else to foot the bill. His idol had been Frank Sinatra.

I heard a few years later that he had married an heiress to the "Don the Beachcomber" fortune, which had not lasted long after they had moved to Florida. I had thought to myself, "What a good place for him." All those lonely widows needed someone to share their last hurrah with—a perfect fit for him. But the tables had turned. They had the money, and he had to work for it. Sweet revenge. Although he always had his ways to make it seem as if he were guiding the show, he could never hold on to anyone. Those rich widows had ironclad wills drawn up with their children and families protected. He would see none of their assets when they were gone. Of course, I am only supposing this. It seems like what he would do; it is the only game he knew.

I did get word from a mutual friend in the last couple of years that he had returned to LA at some point and was living with failing health in a senior assisted-living home—one for the indigent. His kids had no money, and I know they had no feelings of responsibility. After all, he had never been responsible for them. One of his daughters had once told me that their song had been "Papa Was a Rolling Stone," because wherever he laid his hat was his home. That was Vern. I hope she was at his bedside when he died later that year. Some tiny spark of the Cygnus I fell in love with still lies sheltered in a deep, hidden pocket in my heart. I wish him well on his way.

I recently re-connected with Lacy and Sally through social media. They have made new lives for themselves, returning to the mainland and having families, still the tight-knit bunch of sisters that they always were.

Since Lacy had taken over the apartment and "the book" (my list of client phone numbers), she was able to do whatever she wanted, including whatever she chose with Vern. I never asked what happened afterward because I didn't really want to know. Something inside holds a morbid curiosity, but I leave those dogs asleep.

But Yahowha will always be like a guardian angel to me. He visits me in my dreams occasionally, and we have a good chat or just sit together. I know he is proud of the strong woman I have become because of the look of love and compassion radiating from his eyes.

△ ▽ △ ∀

On my last day in Honolulu, Mother and I took a cab to the airport. I asked the driver to take the long way around Sand Island, not the freeway. I wanted to take in every view, every smell of this love I was about to bid aloha to: the scent of the sea as we drove along the ocean's edge, the aroma of pineapple being processed at the Dole Cannery, and the essence of plumeria, pikake, puakenikeni, and tuberose wafting from the lei stands at the airport. I wanted to remember that combined essence of a tropical city at the ocean's shore on an island in the middle of a vast sea filled with sunshine baking everyone into a state of aloha. Mahalo, Hawaii, for giving me the gifts of your heart, sharing your cleansing blue waters, and allowing me to learn my lessons and move on. For keeping me safe. You will never be forgotten. *A hui hou*, I shall return to you whole.

Epilogue

Why do I tell this story now? I have grown up and lived quite a life on my upward spiral, wearing many hats and maintaining my independence. I know there are many who lived through those times and can relate to what I went through, as they have gone through their own varied journeys. Those born later may not realize what really did happen back in those days, and I know that no little girl will ever live the life I have.

I was told that when I grew up, I would get married to a nice man, have a family, and be comfortable. Not rich, but not wanting. My parents always wished the best for me and would gently guide me. I say gently because I was so explosive regarding anything that was not my idea. My mother says I was born with a mission. I always seemed to have an agenda, some curiosity to explore, or an event to create. I was passionate about everything I endeavored to do, and they did not want to quell that passion, although they had no unrealistic expectations that I would someday become a rocket scientist or get involved in politics.

When I was in kindergarten, I wanted to be a ballerina, but then I decided I would rather be a nurse. It was very typical stuff till I found out what the possibilities were. Bob Dylan says, "You don't come into this life to find out who you are. You come into this life to make yourself into something." That is truly the narrative of my generation. Freedom was something we thought we had when I was growing up, but as women, we did not. We were raised as cookie-cutter copies of our mothers, yet my generation broke that mold and would go on to demand equality and command respect. As children, we had the freedom to leave our houses after breakfast and were trusted to handle ourselves in ways that parents do not bestow on their children today.

Maybe that is why we were brave enough to blaze the trails we did. So I took the risks, seized my opportunities, and had the experiences to know what I did and did not want to do.

I finally met a man worthy of my love, and I his. But that is another story that happened later in life. And because we have no children, I feel this story is my legacy. I care deeply about it. It must be told today because tomorrow, it will be fiction.

After I returned to Chicago, I would receive a card from Ted, my taxi-driver friend, every year for my birthday and sometimes on Valentine's Day. They would have roses on them and be often collaged from other cards, with savings bonds in fifty- or hundred-dollar denominations tucked inside them when he could afford it. This went on for about fifteen years, and I held onto them till they matured only a few years ago. The cards stopped containing the bonds at some point, and then the cards stopped coming altogether, but the same sentiment was always there. "Dawn, I love you. You are beautiful. Your friend, Theodore Yonamine." I did not know what became of him, but recently a dear friend did some digging and found that he died in 2017.

I still maintain a few Source Family ties, though they seem to have dwindled over time as our differences have continued to separate us. I miss the sisters who do not relate to me, anymore, and I still hold a place for them in my heart. We maintain a Facebook group to check in now and again, but everyone has veered off on their own paths. Many have become successful; some just get by. Surprisingly, Isis and I have become quite good chums, and I have become an adored auntie to her daughter Saturna. Isis needles me to get my story out, and we discuss the important issues of life as it smacks us in the face with a future we never expected. In fact, when she and Electricity began compiling information, stories, and pictures for their book, *The Legend of Father and the Source Family*, I helped do research and brainstorm with them. I also keep in touch with Harvest Moon, who is now Electricity's wife. They have a successful real-estate business on Kauai, three sons, and a growing passel of grandchildren.

Of course, I am also Auntie to my brother's four girls and my sister's only daughter, Alana. My nieces look at me as their eccentric Auntie Dawn and take me with a few grains of salt. It is hard to explain to them who I really am, and I do not think they really want to know. They have been raised with entirely different standards.

As for the further adventures of Dawn, the plan is to keep writing. I had a good time when I returned to Chicago during the punk-rock and new-wave era of music. And I subsequently did become a clothing designer, eventually returning to my beloved Hawaii to open a metaphysical bookstore and café and to make myself new again and again. Today I reside on the Big Island and enjoy waking up with the birds, fresh air, and flora and fauna of the tropics.

And the love of my life, Stephen.

Dawn & Stephen

Did you enjoy my story?
Please leave your thoughts and reviews on
Goodreads and Amazon

Acknowledgments

My deepest thanks are extended to Adam Sydney for constantly facing me with my writing demons and patiently guiding me toward the answers to the hard questions. My writing cohorts, Liz Peck, Shaku Huffman, Rose Haywood, Nancy Rogers, and Karen Kuester, have gently coaxed me into reflection during our weekly critiques. I am grateful to my mother and sister, Amy, who have always been there for me. While they do not always agree with me, they are the first ones to stand at my side in battle. Also, Cheryl Lansker for being the best Beta reader and helping with my launch, MAHALO. And to my husband, Stephen Ridsdale, for being supportive, egging me on, and not judging my experiences, thank you.

Isis

When Isis joined the Source Family at twenty-nine years of age, she was already older than most of us, except for Yahowha. She had had the privilege of having been acquainted with Jim Baker before he had taken the names of Father Yod and Yahowha. With a slew of life experiences under her belt, she was her own person. When she saw Yahowha's vision, she had to join him on this incredible ride with the Source Family.

Already working in photography, she took on the role of Family documentarian and began to record as much about our experience as possible, with a passion. She taped all of our morning classes and compiled scrapbooks of the photos she had captured, as well as saving many mementos along the way. They are now all neatly stashed at the UCSB Hamilton Library.

Some accused her of being obsessed, and I even had a strong dislike for her at several key moments in my life. But lots of water has passed under that bridge, and it is stronger than ever. I remain one of her closest friends. Many have wanted to publish their adventures with the Source Family, but Isis is the one who did it first. Everyone went on with their own lives, but she stuck to her purpose. Of course, she had lots of help along the way from Electricity and Harvest Edmonds, Jodi Wille, Maria Demopoulos, and Yours Truly. But she is the one who got it done.

Without the care and rabid possession she has shown for our Family records and memorabilia, they would have never survived as such a comprehensive collection. In fact, she went dumpster-diving at one point when Yahowha instructed us to throw everything away in his zeal to teach us to be unattached to the material. Today we have a set of recordings of many of his classes, which Isis had restored by Karl Anderson—some of which even helped inspire me with my memories. With her unequaled photo library taken by various Family members, including herself, of most of the Family's journey, she has kindly shared many of the images I have included in this book.

Thank you, Isis, for being there as a friend and spiritual sister, encouraging me to keep on, being there to nudge my memories, and acting as our Dragon Lady Record Keeper.

Galaxy & Isis

All photos from the Source Family time are used with the kind permission of The Source Family Archives, University of Santa Barbara Hamilton Library Special Editions.

Additional photos are by Dawn Hurwitz or The Hurwitz Family

Travelers to Rainbow Gathering used with the kind permission of Gary Raffanti

Thank you to Timothy Miller for allowing me to use some copy from his work "The 60s Communes, Hippies and Beyond in the preface of my work.

About Dawn

Born with a fierce sense of independence and curiosity in Chicago, Dawn departed on a journey at sixteen to discover The Source Family commune in LA California. They traveled to Hawaii where she remained with them for five years as a wife of Father Yod and a council member until 1977.

Returning to Chicago in 1979, she spent a decade in clothing and costume design while rubbing elbows with the music community. Her forthcoming book "Remnants' will highlight all her exciting 80s adventures.

Her heart-strings to Hawaii pulled her back in 1989 when she created a metaphysical bookstore cafe called "huna ohana" on the Big Island of Hawaii her home. In the early 2000s, a new transformation blossomed, this time as an Apple Tech.

Now retired and sharing a home named Avoland with her husband Stephen and their beloved cats. A third memoir is in the works covering that era.

Dawn and author/educator Adam Sydney began The Puna Writers Workshops in 2017 prompting her to finally scribble down all of her stories.

Find Dawn on:

Facebook, Instagram, Linked-In, http://www.dawnhurwitz.com